1948
THE PORSCHE
50TH ANNIVERSARY BOOK
1998

FANTASTIC PORSCHE

Photographs by Peter Vann

With written contributions by Clauspeter Becker, Emanuel Eckardt, Michael Köckritz, Rolf Kunkel, Jürgen Lewandowski, Heinz Prüller, David Staretz, Rico Steinemann, Herbert Völker and Helmut Zwickl

AURUM PRESS

IN MEMORY OF

Professor Dr. Ing. h.c.

Ferdinand "Ferry" Porsche

September 19, 1909 – March 27, 1998

MEN OF TASTE AND EXPERIENCE CAN APPRECIATE THE DIFFERENCE: Women without war paint – natural beauty as opposed to styled visual effect. Cars present themselves in a very similar way, in smooth paint and hard chrome or through the fascination of a roaring engine and vibration. Peter Vann, the extravagant Parisian photographer, has clearly chosen the appeal of the exterior.

That impresses me. From an up-close perspective, the history of the Porsche sportscar marque appears to be an adventure in development and technology, a transition from the hand-made mid-engined roadsters of the early days to the perfection of modern volume production; a mutation from the beginning at the design office in Gmünd, Austria (in the appealing setting of a former saw mill), to the automobile manufacturing and developing company renowned throughout the world. It is all too easy for the big picture to slip into the background. Peter Vann never lost sight of the big picture. It is his visual gift for capturing the great lines that makes him so outstanding – and that is exactly what this survey of the past 50 years is meant to be.

It might be the Porsche focus on top intellectual performance that turns the hunt for the pure spirit into a passion – and led me to work with Peter Vann. He showed me that cars can be brought to life without ever turning the ignition key. Whereas my enthusiasm for technology exhausts itself in the written word, he seeks out the reflective beauty of the mobile ambience. Nevertheless, a principle of physics teaches us that all invested energy remains unchanged, even when the individual portions shift, and therefore the quiet sensuality of his photographs must stand in contrast to the considerable dynamism with which they were created.

That too is professional experience: for instance, when the crane meant to serve as the high perch for the camera sinks into the sand of a Normandy beach before the pictures of the Cisitalia-Porsche can be taken. Or the story he told me of how, years ago, when tied tight to the top of the mast, his boat capsized in the stormy South Italian sea. He nearly drowned and the camera was eaten up by the salt water, but he saved the film with the pictures – taken from a new and adventurous tilted position! There are reasons enough to follow his perspective – for me (as someone whose approach to the fascination of technology is tinged with respect), and for him (as a pure man of the eye) – in order to retrace the heritage of Porsche.

Anton Hunger
Public Relations and Press Department, Dr. Ing. h.c. F. Porsche AG

First published 1998 by Aurum Press Ltd, 25 Bedford Avenue, London WC1B 3AT.

Copyright © Praetor und Rindlisbacher Verlagsgesellschaft mbH Reutlingen

A catalogue record for this book is available from the British Library

ISBN 1 85410 601 5

Printed in Germany

Designed and produced by Praetor und Rindlisbacher Verlagsgesellschaft mbH Reutlingen

Concept, graphic design, and overall realization: Uli Praetor
Conceptual consultant: Herbert Völker
English translation: Colin Brazier
Typesetting: Speedy Typer Desktop Publishing GmbH
Lithography: Laudert/Vreden, Unternehmen für innovative Medientechnik
Printing: Offsetdruckerei Karl Grammlich GmbH, Pliezhausen
Binding: Buchbinderei Sigloch, Künzelsau

PORSCHE

by Eberhard von Kuenheim

WHAT CAN HAVE INSPIRED SOMEONE only shortly after Germany's destruction in the Second World War to risk building up a new existence as a manufacturer of sports cars? This of all things, at a time when the country was in ruins and mobility meant owning a bicycle or waiting interminably for the streetcar to come along. What confidence, what unlimited trust in the future must have possessed Ferry Porsche in 1948, at the age of 39, when he created and built the first sports car bearing the family name? Germany was just introducing its new currency, and many Germans were discovering after a lengthy interval what they wanted from life, but to be honest, did their ambitions run to ownership of a sports car? What far-sighted vision, what creative spark must have entered into Ferry Porsche in those dark days? What passion, not to say bravado, what obsessive faith in individual mobility must have driven him on?

Only someone with a mission, holding fast to a deep-seated conviction, could have made such a decision as this. Only a visionary businessman could have put it into practice. Schumpeter, the economist, once said that the true businessman's "thoughts must dwell on the future," and we can imagine Ferry Porsche's desire to transform the design office established by his father in 1931 into a genuine automobile manufacturing operation. His name must stand together with many pioneering German businesspeople from the immediate post-war period: Josef Neckermann and Willy H. Schlieker, Max Grundig and Heinz Nixdorf. They are the figureheads of the German economic miracle. Yet Ferry Porsche must be placed in a separate category even from these notable personalities, whose names are now almost forgotten outside of Germany: his life's work has survived in all its splendor, and now stands proudly there for all to see.

It's unlikely that Ferry Porsche would have approved of this brief summary: his role was always that of the "son of the company's founder," never that of the founder himself. It is true to say that his father, the legendary automobile designer and "inventor" of the people's car, the Volkswagen Beetle, did indeed lay the foundation stone for the later sports-car company. But the edifice erected on this foundation stone today is Ferry Porsche's work. ("Ferry", incidentally, was the local-style nickname for a child who had been named Ferdinand Anton Ernst at birth, but who retained this affectionate abbreviated form of address in adult life.) All he took over from his father was a small engineering design office: it was under his guidance that the Porsche company became the great name in sports cars that it is today.

We must assume that Ferry Porsche was already an "entrepreneur" at the time when he decided to produce his own sports car, and that he remained an entrepreneur of the most visionary kind in later life. His constant aim was to implement lasting values for his company, and it is probable that the fashionable term "shareholder value" would have scarcely raised a smile. For him, short-term reactions have never generated lasting strength, and indeed a "short-sighted" proprietor would never have created such a company and ensured its survival.

Ferry Porsche guided the company successfully through many of severe automobile industry crisis and through equally difficult internal management situations. He chose to decline all offers to buy the company out, so that Porsche remains independent to this day. With a gentle but determined touch, Ferry Porsche initially held the management reins in his own hands. When diverging interests in the families who own the company threatened to become a problem in the early 1970s, he appointed outside managers to take his own place. Later, when rumors of fresh crisis situations were rife, he exerted his influence to maintain a peaceful and cool-headed atmosphere. He urged the family to live up to their work and their name, and to keep going in tough situations.

Yet Ferry Porsche always avoided making a big show. He did not seek the spotlight, but worked backstage – and all the more effectively there. Modesty is one of his most notable traits of character. Without much ado or undue pressure, but with tremendous clarity, he has determined the varied fate of the company that bears his name.

For Ferry Porsche, the company was always in the foreground, never himself. At first, he led as the "gentle boss" (as the German media named him in 1961). Later, as Chairman of the Supervisory Board, he guided Porsche as a family company from a position in the background – and brought it from that position onto the stock market when this was deemed necessary. He was still something of a "final court of appeal," even though he resigned from his position as Chairman of the Supervisory Board back in 1990. His connection with the company as honorary chairman remained until his death on March 27, 1998.

The way that Ferry Porsche influenced the company was seldom visible to the public. He is not known for great words; the greatness of his life's work can be seen in the fact that his company has remained independent until this day.

At the time of writing this independence appears more stable then ever: for the company now maintains close relationships and cooperates with all three big German automotive corporations – Mercedes, Volkswagen, and BMW. Porsche is today a highly respected development partner for nearly every automobile company in the world – a policy of Bismarckian brilliance.

This form of cooperation has only become possible as a consequence of the Porsche company's outstanding skill in product development. Its history (with its roots as a design office) offers only a partial explanation for this reputation. After development of the first Porsche car, Ferry Porsche quickly realized that the new company would be too small to acquire enough work for (and above all, the ability to finance) a large, powerful development team. But he also realized that there could be no lasting strength without precisely this kind of innovative development team. Ferry Porsche knew that of all companies, Porsche was and is totally de-

pendent on outstanding engineering, that Porsche was particularly attractive for technical people and engineering economists – and must remain so. The ingenious solution to this problem was to set up a company that would work for other companies – in nearly every country in the world. The strategy was successful, because hardly any other company in the automotive trade regarded Porsche as a competitor for their own product – and some simply wanted to adorn themselves with the "Developed by Porsche" seal.

For the development team – and also for the reputation of the Porsche marque – there was another step that played a crucial role: participation in motor racing. Porsche entered its cars in nearly every discipline – and was nearly always successful. For the engineers, the task itself was even more important than the success: to build a team that, in little or no time, could push development forward under almost unbearable pressure. In a team like this, decisions are made quickly – it learns to bear the heaviest of loads. For a development company, as Porsche (among other things) is, participation in motor sport is one of the best management schools.

Thus, Porsche became something of an "institution of higher education" for the entire automotive industry. Today, engineers who spent time at Porsche in the course of their career can be found in positions of leadership in nearly every company in this industry. Ferry Porsche took this in his stride – maybe even with a certain sense of satisfaction. For the reputation that Porsche enjoys today throughout the automotive world is certainly due in no small part to this silent "infiltration" of the industry with Porsche engineers.

*The senior man himself – who was called "junior" all his life – made many a decisive contribution to the reputation of his company and his engineers. Even in very satisfactory times, he resisted the temptation to appear self-satisfied. Restraint in good times generated credit for phases of heavy strain. "Porsche never cared to be appreciated just because his name was Porsche," wrote **auto motor und sport** magazine for his seventieth birthday.*

German industry owes a lot to Ferry Porsche: He created – and sustained – a fascinating automobile marque with an international reputation. With his passion for sports cars, Porsche helped this type of car gain acceptance all over the world. And he built up a company that again and again produced very attractive cars which never followed short-term fashions. He designed a marque that is today a world-wide symbol for German engineering skill. He confronted whole generations of engineers with tremendous challenges; trained them for the entire industry – and showed that modesty and success do not have to be contradictory terms.

CONTENTS

CHAPTER 1

Visions

50 years of sports car manufacturing in Stuttgart make up precisely half the Porsche story.

In 1898, Ferdinand Porsche had his first clear ideas on how to improve the automobile. At the age of 23, the apprentice metal worker who had been lured out of his Bohemian village by the burgeoning wonder of electricity, had found his profession: automobile designer.

As the century came to a close, it was a profession without an instruction manual, without regulations, without courses, and without any store of experience on which to draw. It was a good time to realize that vision is a designer's natural perspective.

LOHNER-PORSCHE
Straight into the automotive hall of fame with this first piece of work as a young man

AUSTRO DAIMLER SASCHA
A quarter of a century and an innumerable number of inventions later: the first hint of a car for the people, but first it needed a Count as godfather

At Night, When the Horses Didn't Shy

by Herbert Völker

Lohner-Porsche

THE DATE IS CERTAIN: June 26, 1898. Ferdinand Porsche made a good impression on that day during technical support for a test drive. He was skilful, clever when it came to improvising, and not yet even 23 years old.

We are also certain of the roads upon which the test drive was performed (along with innummerable later drives), and nearly all of the buildings are still standing: stately, beautiful residences of the bourgeoisie, proudly untouched, as though there had never been any bomb damage.

We are in Vienna. The most famous part of the test route is the *Berggasse*, for Sigmund Freud himself held consultations in house number 19, and today, the Freud Museum is visited by almost as many tourists as the National Opera House, which is only partly due to the fact that it has longer visiting hours.

THE COUCH, the legendary one, was located in one of the rooms at the back of the house, so it was possible to accelerate a motor car flat out when reaching Berggasse 19, without hindering the blossoming of a young science. So there is no need to imagine that thoughts like "That Porsche and his wagon are really getting on my nerves" could have delayed the development of psychoanalysis.

Full power was needed when the car got to house number 19, because just a bit later a slight incline began, steepening sharply a block later until the *Währingerstrasse* was reached. Thus, the Berggasse, which means "hill street" in German, lived up to its name, and from 1898 to 1905 it was the standard by which all climbing power was measured on Ferdinand Porsche's equipment.

On that June day in the year 1898, the contraption ran quietly (since it had an electric motor), but it did not run well. It did not even make it up the small incline of the *Börsegasse* as it headed towards *Ringstrasse*. Porsche had a few suggestions for quick modifications (he was not responsible for the design itself), and he was allowed to make them. Then the time came for another run at the *Berggasse*, and from then on it happened again and again, of course at night, when the horses didn't shy.

At the bottom of the valley, where the *Berggasse* gains momentum, the Lohner company's building stood on the corner of *Porzellangasse*. Today the house can be seen in all its renovated glory, and we are fast approaching our subject.

What was the 23 year old Ferdinand Porsche like in the year 1898? "Small, inconspicuous" according to the biographers. Introverted, "fearless," but also "with dreamy eyes." Eyes which were being followed more and more often by a young lady accounts clerk named Aloisia. Readers with some expertise may guess: Here, a dynasty is about to be founded – with far-reaching consequences. First, however, for the vehicle with wheel-hub drive.

Back home in the Bohemian village of Maffersdorf, Porsche had learned metal working in his father's workshop, but his fanatical interest in electricity that took him away from this predestined trade and the countryside. He joined the Viennese electrical company Béla Egger (where Brown Boveri had its origins) and learned right away to wield a broom and lubricate drive belts.

14 ▪ 1

The steel commutator cover as a pictorial symbol of this century's technology. Running uphill from the Lohner Building in Vienna is an aptly named road: the Berggasse. At Number 19 on the right, just after the traffic light, Siegmund Freud shrank his first heads while Ferdinand Porsche, passing by, selected a lower gear

It is easy to imagine how the hierarchy in the company back then must have treated an apprentice from the country. Young Porsche's character must have been exceptional for him to become head of the testing bay in just four years. As the Egger company delivered the motor for a Lohner electric car project, the test drives mentioned earlier began about then, and the young man drew attention to himself. A year later he changed sides, since the curve of innovation clearly ran through Lohner's workshops.

Lohner was an old-fashioned, reputable company for the manufacture of coaches and wagons, operating on the basic assumption that "the Kaiser would always be pulled by four horses." Alongside that, however, there was plenty of room (and even considerable capital) for new ideas. Ludwig Lohner was one of the great visionaries with the talent of an Emil Jellinek (Mercedes), but he operated on the solid ground of a mature company and without the latter's magic touch.

Lohner was convinced that the automobile had a future, even though at the time it was news in Germany and particularly in France, but not in the Austro-Hungarian Empire. He traveled around to get the big picture, make contacts, and find a partner for engines. He was just as aware of the disadvantages of the electric motor as most of us are a hundred years later. He persistently attempted to find a German or French gasoline-powered engine. As an alternative, he even approached Rudolf Diesel with the idea "You ought to put a Diesel engine in an AUTOMOBILE!" but he was twenty years too early for that concept.

In short: When Ferdinand Porsche began working for the Lohner company in 1899, he had not joined any old manufacturer of horsedrawn coaches, but one with many a bright idea that, for a short time, harmonized with the young genius. Since after several attempts it became clear that it was not possible to get hold of a decent gasoline-powered engine, at least not at short notice in 1899, a new electric had to take its place. A job for Ferdinand.

At the time of his job switch, Porsche already had plans for a wheel-hub motor. He was able to realize it within three months, after the patent rights had been secured. The basic idea for the system had come into the world earlier in England (without having worked in practice), and Lohner and Porsche were aware of this. Porsche succeded in realizing the concept, and had the further idea of putting the motors on the front wheels, which were now once and for all be given the task of steering. (The '98 test vehicle had had rear-wheel steering, which worked about as well as one would imagine; it was a ludicrous debacle).

Front-wheel drive was not exactly new at the time either, but it was still rather exotic. The combination of the two unusual concepts (wheel-hub motor and front-wheel drive) was exciting, innovative (direct drive, no intermediate gears), and also full of detail problems, which allowed the designer and inventor in Ferdinand Porsche to come to the surface for the first time. He was 24 years old.

The steerable wheel-hub motor and the complete elimination of a transmission were not the only features now revealed for the first time. The Lohner-Porsche *Elektromobil*, as it was now called officially, was also the first car in the world with brakes on all four wheels. Besides the normal band brake on the rear wheels, the electric motors provided automatic braking on the front wheels.

A handwheel was used to select six forward speeds, reverse, and the three brake settings via the selector drum (controller).

Porsche's internal-pole motor was mounted directly on the axle. The motor housing formed the wheel hub and rotated on ball bearings around the star-shaped magnet, which was affixed to the end of the axle. Each motor developed 2.5 horsepower at 120 revolutions per minute. A 44-cell accumulator with a capacity of up to 300 ampere-hours delivered a current of up to 80 volts. This configuration permitted a top

16 ▪ 1
The name Lohner is stands for a dynasty of Austrian tradition, and also for innovation. Joining up with a man like Ludwig Lohner put the 23-year old Ferdinand Porsche, who had come to Vienna as a metal worker and learned to be an electrician, on a fast career track

16 ▪ 1

17 ▪ 1
The factory was already on the outskirts of the city; Porzellangasse 2 was the headquarters and starting point for the test-drive circuit

17 ■ 1

18 ▪ 1

Stub axle, protective plate, and the six carbon brushes. Apart from the sheer weight of the wheel that had to be removed, the wearing parts (the rate of wear depending more or less on starting and braking habits) were relatively easy to reach

18 ▪ 2

In the current phase of restoration and conservation, the car in the photographs on these pages, which belongs to the Viennese Museum of Technology, has wooden wheels with a tread layer; originally, solid-rubber tires were used

18 ▪ 1

18 ▪ 2

Wheel with permanently attached coils (armatures), commutator, and protective steel cover. The commutator had to be kept as free as possible from dust and grease – probably a relatively easy matter thanks to the large cover. The complete front wheel weighed about 100 kilograms (220 pounds)

19 ▪ 1

20·1

20 ■ 1

*A racing version with all-wheel
drive and batteries weighing
1,800 kg (3,968 lb) was built in the
Fall of 1900 at the request of an
English customer.*

*It is alleged to have reached
90 km/h (56 mph), but made no
impression on the motor racing
scene. Before handing over of the
car in Vienna, Service Manager Pöll
is seen at the wheel with Ferdinand
Porsche next to him and a senior
clerk from the Lohner company
on the back seat*

21 ■ 1

*The Lohner coach factory
during conversion to
automobile manufacturing*

21 ■ 1

speed of 50 km/h (31 mph); the "normal speed" was 35 km/h (22 mph), at which it was possible to travel a distance of 50 kilometers (31 miles). You can decide for yourself how long you think it took to charge the batteries: historical sources vary from one half hour to two hours, and one might suspect that it took even longer. Lohner, with impressive foresight, offered a kind of after-sales support before even the first dozen cars had been sold (which took two years).

Highly effective as the motors were (since the power was created right where it was needed), the problem of weight remained. The first model's accumulator weighed 410 kilograms (904 lb), and each motor 115 kg (254 lb), which adds up to 640 lb (1,411 lb) for the drive alone. The coachwork itself weighed just 340 kg (750 lb), which permitted an overall weight below one thousand kilograms (2,200 lbs), which is definately within the "modern" range. Not quite as modern, however, was the weight of one front wheel – 100 kg (220 lb) or more. Changing a tire was no easy job!

As the car with wheel-hub engine came into existence in 1899, the year 1900 is often mentioned as its premiere year, because of its impressive debut at the World Exhibition in Paris that year. The car was the sensation of the show and returned with all conceivable laurels. Thus, with his very first design, Ferdinand Porsche entered the century as a young star of the automobile world.

From England came the question as to whether the car could not also be equipped with four motors for racing. Why not? The rear wheels were much easier anyway. With stronger motors, the car needed no less than 1,800 kg (3,968 lb) of battery weight. Nevertheless, the design took off at this point, since with four wheels of the same size, the car lost the"coach" character due mainly to the high rear wheels.

For Porsche, putting motors on the remaining wheels (during 1900) was child's play. Later, when permanent four-wheel drive finally became relevant on world markets, historians would say: "Porsche did it eighty years ago."

The Vienese newspaper "Allgemeine Automobil Zeitung" was invited for a short test drive. The report recapitulates the technology once more: the fixed star-shaped magnet, the rotating armature, which "causes the wheel to turn. In other words, there is no outside power source via some kind of transmission. Simultaneously it is also a steered wheel that, like a horse, pulls the car in the direction in which is steered. A brilliant idea, executed with decided skill. On Porsche-Lohner automobiles, all the power-wasting gears normally mounted between the engine and the car's wheels have become superfluous. The driver directs energy directly from the battery to the car's wheels, without wastefully scattering its wattage to the four winds."

"Electric motors are known for their choleric temperament; they are sprinters. On other systems, speed reduction is the method used to combat this undesirable trait. On the Lohner-Porsche design, the motor is the car wheel itself, which runs just as fast as the motor rotates."

"It was necessary, therefore, to reduce the speed of rotation to a level suitable for the task at hand, while retaining the highest possible propulsive force, which alone guarantees the car's speed on inclines. A difficult task, accomplished brilliantly by Mr. Lohner and Mr. Porsche."

The driver's impressions were clearly dominated by the sense of comfort (other body styles were already available as an alternative to the original "chaise" from the previous year): "In the completely noiseless, softly sprung, and comfortably upholstered Lohner-Porsche automobiles, you feel as if you are on a ship rather than a car. The sensation is one of gentle gliding, not the rolling motion you feel in a Ford."

The author has more to add: The "extremely elegant vehicles" are sprung so softly and so comfortably upholstered, "that the occupants regularly inspire onlookers to jealousy." The spatial layout is also praised: everything is "well-balanced, with nowhere a clumsy, square battery box to give reason for criticism."

Although the "market" in Austria-Hungary was still nearly non-existent, Lohner and Porsche expanded their product line withing months: there were three body versions (followed later by a truck and a bus), and two more powerful motors (up to seven horsepower per wheel, up to twelve for trucks).

Converted to today's purchasing power, the initial cost for a typical Porsche-Lohner model would be somewhere in the region of 70,000 German Marks. To drive it 5,000 kilometers a year would cost about 9,000 Marks for the chauffeur and 5,000 for batteries and recharging. To this would come an astonishing 25,000 Marks for tires, if you had already made the switch from wood or solid-rubber to the new but still puncture-prone pneumatic technology.

Despite all this, the automobile had excellent prospects: coaches and horses were not cheap either, coachmen's wages were hardly lower than for chauffeurs, horses ate a lot more than an accumulator. And tire prices could be expected to tumble soon.

What changed the situation even more quickly however, was the comparison between electric cars and those powered by gasoline. Resolution of the delivery crisis for gasoline engines coincided exactly with the turn of the century, after which the electric motor reverted to the role of a temporary emergency solution. We can take distinct pleasure in the fact that its pros and cons a hundred years ago sounded exactly the same as they do today.

The negative aspects of the electric motor included its higher purchase price, shorter range, high battery weight, and inconvenient charging. Nonetheless, it was still worth dreaming about as "city car" concept, a subject guaranteed to remain topical. Two hours of operation, wrote Ludwig Lohner before the turn of the century, seemed "at first to be terribly short, but experience shows that in city driving, the car stands about more than it moves." Our good friend Lohner seems to have had an eye for the future!

As a businessman still obliged to use the electric motor, Lohner hoped that Vienna would defend itself boldly against the introduction of the gasoline-fueled automobile: "Grant to us 'residents of the World Village' that last little scrap of oxygen and enjoyable ai, that our splendid municipal facilities have left us; for it would be mercilessly ruined by the combustion products from innumerable gasoline-powered engines."

Lohner's enthusiasm for ecology disolved the moment that reasonable gasoline engines were again available, and Porsche favored the best of all worlds anyway.

We can sense the breathless pace of technological development: in the same year as the much acclaimed show in Paris, in 1900, the year in which four-wheel drive was developed, Porsche also built a hybrid car. It retained the wheel-hub motors and thus direct drive, one of the the main advantages of the "Paris motor car" (at that time transmissions were a tremendous problem and a horror for manufacturers and chauffeurs alike).

Two De-Dion Bouton gasoline engines drove dynamos, which recharged the battery and/or supplied the front-wheel motors directly with power. This was the basis for the "Mixte" model. Over the years, the gasoline side of this vehicle became more and more significant, particularly once the Mercedes engine was available.

We are still speaking of Porsche as a very young man, only in his mid-twenties. He had already discovered his love of motor sport, and before the year 1900 was out the second half of the legend began .

No wonder later historical novelists felt called to recreate this in their imagination and to add interest by bringing Fräulein Aloisia, the clerk from the Egger company, into the story:

"He roared onto the scene, flying around the corners of the hillclimb on the *Semmering* pass. Number 6, the Lohner *Elektromobil*. It was obviously the fastest. And such cornering!"

"'Porsche!' the crowd shouted."

"The man who sat behind the steering wheel like a little faun, drove like the devil. He scarcely seemed human at all, but rather a piece of this *Elektromobil,* which – despite its tremendous speed, clung to the track like a limpet."

"Standing alone on a straight section of the road, a young lady waved. The driver did not lift his eyes from the road for as much as a moment."

"That evening Vienna's newspaper boys cried out on the streets: 'Extra, extra, read all about it! Lohner's motor race record!'"

"Aloisia Johanna pressed her hands against her chest, against the newspaper she held to her bodice. She would not read it until she got home. Her eyes were moist."

What can still make our eyes moist today, is the terse determination with which Ferdinand Porsche also came to be his company's first works driver; the way he viewed motor sport as a natural element in his life and career; the way he relentlessly persued it in all conceivable guises, and how his principles prevailed all the way to the other end of the century.

Despite the (never conclusively proven) capability of the four-motor version of the Lohner-Porsche electric motor car to reach a speed of 90 km/h (56 mph), the Mixte was the better vehicle for racing. Porsche recognized this quickly and personally brought home victory in the 1902 Exelbergrennen (and others). The metal worker who had become an electrician evidently had no problems with gasoline, the new fuel.

Archduke Franz Ferdinand called for a Lohner-Porsche Mixte as his personal transport for the 1902 Emperor's maneuvers, and Ferdinand Porsche was his chauffeur. All three came through with colors held high.

Lohner-Porsche chassis with wheel-hub motors were later used for light "chaises" and heavy commercial vehicles. The fire engines were particularly popular, and remained in existence until the 1930s. Nevertheless, Ludwig Lohner's company and the young designer's free spirit drifted slowly apart until Ferdinand Porsche left to become Technical Director at Austro Daimler in 1906.

Before that, however, the matter with the Fräulein from the Egger company's office had to be settled. Ferdinand Porsche married Aloisia Johanna Kaes on October 17, 1903. The honeymoon brought them to Salzburg, to Lake Garda, and (what a coincidence!) to Nice, where Mr. Jellinek had some important questions concerning the "Mercedes-Electrique" project.

Upon returning to Vienna the young pair moved into an appartment at Berggasse 6. This is precisely the point where the last steep section of the Berggasse begins. No engineer could have taken up quarters closer to the action. Today there is a pizzeria there, and the Berggasse is a one-way street in the downhill direction: a classic brake test route, so to speak.

Daughter Luise was born in 1904 and baby Ferdinand saw the light of day on September 19, 1909, just as father returned with the Semmering hillclimb victor's trophy.

History was, as usual, taking its course.

FERDINAND,
WE'RE GOING TO ITALY!

by Herbert Völker

"COUNT KOLOWRAT, in a great mood as always, made some excellent jokes, which even caused Mr. James F.J. Archibald to laugh – despite the fact that he did not speak German."

From this rally report of 1910 we can see that the good Count was already quite a charismatic figure in his younger years (at 25 in this case). The car that would later bear his name ("Sascha" being short for Alexander), was an up-beat machine, agile and charming.

Ferdinand Porsche created "Sascha" 22 years after the car powered by "wheel-hub motors"; the time that had passed covered nearly half of the designer's creative period, and also corresponded to the share of ideas, designs, inventions, and successes in his life, for from 1898 all the way to his death there were no "down-times," not even a pause in the flow of inspiration.

Here in a few keywords is an outline of this 22-year timespan: Continuation of the "Mixte" technology, first at Lohner, later at Austro Daimler, which caused the paths of Porsche and Jellinek (Mercedes) to cross. A small car called "Maja" (named after Mercedes's youngest sister), then more special sports cars and the discovery of aerodynamics. Victory as driver and designer in the 1910 Prince Henry Run made him something of a media star. Engines for ships and aircraft followed. He served the Austro-Hungarian war machine by providing the most unbelievable transport technologies for the heaviest transport vehicless and guns. The Empire thanked him with high honors, the Institute of Higher Technical Edu-

cation in Vienna made this self-taught mechanic an honorary doctor. After the war was over, as General Manager, he led Austro Daimler to success with a model line in the upper mid-size category.

In the spring of 1921, Ferdinand Porsche was a big boss, but as designer he was just as spontaneous and direct as in the old Berggasse days. He was 45.

His son Ferry, 12 years old, was already driving a two-cylinder two-seater around, not just on the factory grounds in Wiener Neustadt, but also on public roads, whereupon the police just said something like: "Hi, Ferdl."

Another shout, this time a call for the father's services, we will interpret under the laws of poetic license as follows:

"Ferdinand, we're going to Italy."

The speaker is Alexander ("Sascha") Count Kolowrat. After Ludwig Lohner and Emil Jellinek, he was the third extraordinary businessman-cum-car freak with whom Porsche was to have dealings.

Count Kolowrat had all the right ingredients to make him a favorite aristocrat among the Austrians, whether in the days of the old monarchy or in the young republic: ancient lineage, imposing stature, and the sweet charms and excitment of the nobleman's life. There was also his impressively tanned skin: his mother was a Cuban, the daughter of an American cigarette mogul. She had met Kolowrat's father when he, a minister of the monarchy, had been shuffled off rapidly to a faraway land after honorably winning a duel.

Alexander Kolowrat had entered the Austrian automobile

Austro
Daimler

Sascha

28 ▪ 1

28 ▪ 2

28 ▪ 3

28 ▪ 5

28 ▪ 4

28 ▪ 1-4
This relatively common layout for early sports cars had offset seats to provide the driver with elbow room. The little 1100-cc engine developed 45 bhp at a whirling 5,000 rpm. "The steering is jolt-free and self-locking, the steering column is tilted at a sharp angle. The gearshift lever is located in the modern style in the center of the car"

29 ▪ 1

scene as a young sportsman, and was soon known to everyone. The car periodicals reported enthusiastically on the youthful count's drolleries, such as "Blazek's patent cape for Siamese twin sisters" which he introduced at the Alpine run. It was a rain hood for two passengers with two openings for their heads and a shared third opening for hand movements. This was not, however, for steering, since in those days, the rally driver sat in the back with a guest. In the front sat the chauffeur and a race marshal, without any rain protection.

Porsche and Kolowrat had known each other since the pioneering days before the war, when the marshals wished nothing better than to be assigned to the count, who celebrated the climbing of every mountain pass with champagne, and was particularly well known for the cooked meats he always took with him.

The war cannot have caused any serious damage to the remarkable wealth of the Kolowrats (Bohemian glass factories and land), and the young Lord was soon active as a pioneer of the Austrian film industry (the "Sascha" film company) and as a car enthusiast. It was he who must, in the summer of 1921, have said to the General Manager of Austro-Daimler, something like "Ferdinand, we're going to Italy."

We can be doubly certain of this, since Ferry Porsche can remember being picked up from their summer residence on Lake Wörth and being driven to Brescia.

Kolowrat and Porsche wanted to see what was happening on the international car racing scene and, as chance would have it, what they saw was a sensation:

The cars of a certain designer took 1st, 2nd, 3rd, and 4th place; the man already had an international reputation, but not for this kind of high-flying success. He was six years younger than Ferdinand Porsche and his name was Ettore Bugatti.

The modified Model 13 Bugatti that pulled off this four-fold victory was immediately given the nickname "Brescia," a name that became part of car racing history. The race was not for Grand Prix cars, but for the lighter "Voiturettes"; even in this category the Bugatti, with its four valves per cylinder, was a clear indication that small cars were up and coming. Smart, robust and, we should note, completely unlike the familiar species of fragile, spindly cycle-cars.

The mood in which Porsche and Kolowrat spent those days in Italy are unknown, but if we might wish for something like "regained moments," then a video film of that weekend could prove quite satisfying.

We do not know to what degree their fresh thinking overlapped with what they had just experienced, or what effect it had on the designer's vision and the Count's magic touch. Be that as it may: on return, Porsche at once began design work on a new, speedy small car. A marginal note: the "truest of the true," his colleague Karl Rabe, was already involved.

The first concept was a "car for the small man," a four-seater. Probably inspired by the Brescia experience, the idea of marketing the new car through racing soon arose, and so it started life as a two-seater competition version. The 1089-cc engine (with closed aluminum block) had double overhead camshafts driven by spiral bevel gears, and is said to have developed 45 bhp at 5000 rpm; the car weighed 600 kg (1,323 lb).

Kolowrat, who was a member of the Austro Daimler board, supported the financing of the project, probably with private funds as well – a fact which was later reflected in its name: Sascha.

The extent of the Count's personal ambition as a racing driver is now lost in the blur of history. Sascha the man, now in his mid-thirties, was a true film mogul and, as such, had become even more portly – a fact which did nothing to keep him from car racing. He was only aggravated when some of the events required a minimum weight of 120 kg (265 lb). He had no trouble in fullfilling this requirement alone, but was still not allowed to leave the second seat empty. He therefore hit on the idea of carrying a midget as a passenger (at least for hill climbs), which was considered very amusing back then.

The big race selected for the "drum-roll" launch of the Sascha was the 1922 Targa Florio, which was simultaneously Austro Daimler's international racing comeback after the war. The Targa at the peak of its glory, despite its remote Sicilian location, was perhaps the event attracting the most press attention in Europe – at a time when it was considered possible to turn racing prestige into immediate sales success.

General Manager Porsche was no longer available as an active driver, but Count Kolowrat was; the rest of the team was made up of employees from the factory's break-in department: Lambert Pöcher, Fritz Kuhn, and the same Alfred Neubauer who later managed the legendary Silver Arrows.

From Neubauer's memoirs, which were packed with detail, we can deduce (between the lines), that he admired the Count's corpulent appearance, and may have decided to follow his example – with great success, as we know.

Despite the unchanged 1110-cc engine, either as a gag or due to belated entry, Neubauer was allowed to start in the open category, in the midst of the 4.5-liter Mercedes cars. The other Saschas were up against cars in the correct displacement class. The best source that we have here are again Neubauer's memoirs, and the following scene from the Targa Florio is one we would by no means wish to do without:

"The onlookers on the stands are dropping like flies. The people are yelling until they become hoarse. They are waving little flags... A group of German fans is singing 'Wacht um Rhein'. The 'Red Cross' is gathering up dozens of people whose wine consumption has brough them to new depths of unconciousness. At the pit stops, everything is twirling and whirling in chaos." The time has not yet arrived when Alfred Neubauer would lay down the law with his stentorian voice. Everyone still did as they pleased.

Wow! But even Neubauer's style of writing cannot bring the race really to life, perhaps because in the course of the four laps (432 km = 268 miles = nearly eight hours) Neubauer never saw another car. He had been the last one to start, one minute behind a "white elephant" (Lautenschlager's Mercedes). He had no chance, of course, to catch such monsters, nor was he lapped by another car, and he therefore had not the slightest clue as to his own position in the race. It was probably this abstract element in motor racing which caused him to think about providing drivers with signals from the pits, he writes, thus taking the credit for this ingenious idea.

He also declares that that he did not get a bite to eat or a drop to drink throughout the entire eight hours, which is hard to believe when it was "already 30° C (96° F) in the shade at nine o'clock in the morning," but even while he was still alive, nobody contradicted Neubauer.

He writes about the torn-up tires and their chrome leatherer covers from which the wrecked steel bolts flew around his head, about dust and gravel, potholes and craters "like the surface of the moon," and about an eternal "spagetti of curves."

Count Kolowrat dropped out on the first lap, but the three other Saschas reached the finishing line impressively. Kuhn and Pöcher scored a double victory in their class and Alfred Neubauer was another 30 or 40 minutes faster. Due to his entry in a higher category he finished 19th overall in his class, but was "just eight kilometers an hour" (5 mph) slower than the winner.

By all objective standards, this signaled an amazing change in the trend, with the little cars challenging the big ones, and of course we feel something of the "moral victory" too, which aroused strong emotions in the Austrians, humbled in the war – it was their return to international racing. Today, we might call this interpretation of the results "premature historical euphoria."

From the telegrams that were sent and the advertisements that were immediately placed in the newspapers, the Austrians were led to believe that the victory was much grea-

31•1
Back then, "cornering ability" referred more to the driver than the vehicle, with stoic immovability expected from the passenger. This is Alfred Neubauer in the 1922 Targa Florio, with the last start number in the field

32•1
Return of the Targa Florio heros to the Austro Daimler factory in Wiener Neustadt; Neubauer's car is at the front. The boy farthest up front among the onlookers is Ferry Porsche, then twelve and a half years old

32∎1

ter than in actual fact, and Mercedes had to contradict ("the real winner" ... "and without a slide-rule"), since Count Masetti in his "blood red" Mercedes (as opposed to the German-crewed white giants) was the outright winner.

There is a lot of evidence that Ferdinand Porsche, too, "was totally thrilled." It seems that he really enjoyed and celebrated every bit of this success. From today's perspective as well, the Sascha's run in the 1922 Targa Florio marks a trend change in the evolution of motor racing.

In the euphoric mood of the time, racing was the order of the day. An official "racing car" called Sascha, with an engine bored out to 1500 cc was produced, while simultaneously Porsche built two racers of classic size and design. In that hectic year of 1922, there was an impressive chain of Austro-Daimler victories, until suddenly a violent reversal of direction took place.

Fritz Kuhn's fatal crash in a two-liter racing car during the Monza Grand Prix (apparently caused by a wheel fracture) in the Fall of 1922, disturbed Ferdinand Porsche deeply. The sad occasion sharpened the growing crisis between Porsche and his advisory board, which wanted more shareholder value and less enthusiasm for sport.

At that time Austro-Daimler was completely in the hands of Europe's most notorious financial juggler of the time, Camillo Castiglioni. He demanded that the General Manager cooperate in the illegal transfer of foreign currency from export proceeds. Porsche refused and was fired. Months previously the Daimler Motoren Gesellschaft had tried to lure him to Stuttgart, and now he was able to answer the call; in the Spring of 1923 he started the new job.

In light of this turn of events, Sascha, the car, naturally made it as the small man's touring car. Ferdinand Porsche nevertheless liked to refer to it as the Volkswagen's predecesor, and 1100 cubic centimeters invariably seemed to him the right engine size for this type of project.

Count Kolowrat made the world a happier place by discovering a Berlin actress for the movie business, Marlene Dietrich by name. Beyond this, he refreshed the Viennese with a wedding, the likes of which the young republic never saw again: a Russian princess, "a true beauty" was the lucky woman, and Europe's nobility appeared at Stephan's Cathedral as in the days of the Emperor.

This happiness did not last long. Victim of an incurable disease, Sascha Kolowrat died at the age of 42.

CHAPTER 2

Ferry

Ferry Porsche was 38 when he risked the big step towards becoming an independent businessman. Apart from the influence of his genetic heritage, it was the logical evolution of everything he had thought up and created for 15 years at his father's side, but with the distinctive break represented by the independence he now enjoyed.

Development number 356 was not an assignment from the outside, but an active decision (made on June 17, 1947) to design a new product and with it to start a new company, though still without a permanent place of residence. It was a symbol of courage and of belief that there would be light at the end of the tunnel – a striving for freedom which at that time was far from being a matter of course.

Soon, it would become the symbol for the surprised delight with which the future could be experienced and won.

THE MAN
The story of a great creator and motivator, who was able to realize his vision of a sports car to a level of perfection not achieved by anyone else in automotive history

NUMBER 1
*June 1948,
the "icon"*

THE BEGINNING OF ALL THINGS, CHAPTER NO. 356

by David Staretz

356

PORSCHE NUMBER 1 bore the sequential build number 356 within Ferdinand Porsche's design office. That is how simple things are sometimes in history.

Let's page back a few numbers and years: it's 1945, the end of the year. The British Army Major Hirst found an off-road car in Wolfsburg and let it run up against the Jeep in a spirit of technical competition (with success, of course, which led to Hirst organizing an Army production of 917 Volkswagen sedans in the midst of the factory rubble). While this was happening, the engineers who had designed it were fighting for survival in their Carinthian hometown of Gmünd.

The Professor himself was still in French custody, so the office kept itself above water with the oddest of jobs under the leadership of chief engineer Rabe. In exchange for food they repaired plows, threshers and stationary engines. Crack technicians, such as the Carinthian engineer Mickl, who a few years before had produced 188-ton tanks, tractors, and highly complex aerodynamic calculations related to the fastest car in the world (which unfortunately never reached the testing stage), now found themselves building wheelbarrows out of pieces of sheet metal cut from car bodies, with wheels from Maybach tractors.

A year later – Ferdinand's Sohn Ferry had returned from confinement – a promising job arrived from Turin: Commendatore Piero Dusio, General Director of the Cisitalia Works, had examined the future of car racing and found the Porsche team to be the most suitable people for his ambitious project, which also included the design of a farm tractor and a water turbine.

In record time, the engineers drew up plans for a flat-twelve engine with a bore of 56 mm and a displacement of 1,493 cc – good for 10,000 revolutions per minute and at least 300 horsepower. This power unit was to reside in a chrome-molybdenum tubular steel frame. The entire vehicle, including four-wheel drive, would have a dry weight not exceeding 718 kilograms (1,582 lb). Professor Eberan von Eberhorst, formerly of Dresden University, a long-time friend of the company, joined the team to contribute his advanced technological know-how in the material and fuel development areas.

To summarize long suffering in a few words: although the initial model tests were very promising, difficulties with the Italians multiplied. There were problems of communication and, above all, of money. In the end, Dusio was forced to take up an offer from the Argentinian President Peron, to have the sports car plus various farm tractors and trucks built in South America. There the project suffered its final blow, though the Porsche-Dusio car did run for three laps in 1953 with race driver Felice Bonnetto at the wheel. The rest of its history included any amount of dust and rust, before it finally found a home in the Porsche Museum in Zuffenhausen.

Yet in the end, the Cisitalia had done its duty, for there is no question of the fact that it provided the stimulus for the first car that wore the Porsche name.

The professor was in poor physical shape after returning to Gmünd from prisoner-of-war camp, but chief engineer Rabe and Porsche's son Ferry pushed the project ahead.

For a small, light mid-engined two-seater, Volkswagen

38·1

38

components – engine, cable-operated brakes, worm-gear steering, headlights, and various small parts – were the obvious choice. Back then, the road from Gmünd to Wolfsburg was a lot longer than it is today; procuring the parts was extremely tedious and required a sleeve full of tricks.

The qualities of the Volkswagen concept were now reminted as sports-car virtues: a light engine (with no liquid coolant or radiator), a low center of gravity, high durability, and a scanty, streamlined body without ornaments. The engine's central position made it possible to lower the car's nose, which improved its aerodynamics and made it possible for the driver to see the road directly in front of the car. A new tubular steel chassis was developed; it was not until later that a switch was made back to the pressed-steel VW floor assembly.

Careful modification raised the output of the 1,131-cc horizontally opposed engine from 25 to 35 bhp, this being partially due to the increase in compression from 5.8:1 to 7.0:1. With a second downdraft carburetor, it was no problem to obtain 40 bhp, which made top speeds of 135 to 140 km/h (84 to 87 mph) possible thanks to the light, aerodynamic body. To place it in the genuine mid-engined position, the Volkswagen unit was simply turned around, so that the clutch and (unsynchronized) four-speed transmission faced the rear. A typically refreshing example of the straightforward way in which the goal of competitiveness in motor sport was pursued.

At 585 kg (1,290 lb), the designers succeeded it keeping the car very light, which of course favorably affected the braked mass. Even back then a Porsche came to a stop faster than other cars. The chassis and suspension characteristics were not quite as convincing. The decision was made to retain the VW front and rear suspension assemblies including the torsion-bar springs, but somehow they did not harmonize well with the new frame.

Nonetheless, the new car was good enough for its first sports trophy: In July 1948, one month after completion, Herbert Kaes (Ferry Porsche's cousin) won his class in Innsbruck.

NOW FOR THE ARIZONA DREAM: It is six in the morning, on the banks of the Colorado River. The engine of the powerful special truck has been warming up for the past twenty minutes, and now the outlines of the figures finally begin to move. Slowly, like a drawbridge, the loading ramp sinks to reveal a pale shimmer that seeps out of the loading area like the deep sea itself. The loading ramp is pumped up hydraulically, with much clanging of empty metal against metal, clinking of chains, creaking in the cold air. "More light!" somebody called out, which causes two Buicks to move into position with their headlights full on. Slowly, nose forward, the car is pushed onto the special lifting forks almost 10 feet above the ground, the beams from the cars' headlights making it stand out surreally in the morning gloom. The gray shape has a silvery gleam.

Out of place, totally out of place, is all you can think as you look at this scarab from Gmünd here in the far away night, yet as everything becomes brighter in the shadowless light before sunrise, the body poses coolly, its soft, dry curves stand up to the strong contrast of the jagged canyon domes, the tops of which now begin to glow.

The harmony of the design is amazing even down to the minor details. The compact, stocky measurements, the relatively short overhangs, the short wheelbase despite the mid-engine – and still capable of arousing the emotions after all these years : the fresh, clear lines of the hand-beaten aluminum that was given its form by Erwin Kommenda and formed by panel beater Friedrich Weber from Gmünd. It took four days back then before one fender was fully beaten free-handed over a wooden buck, using templates.

Sheet metal was rare and expensive, so the decision to make a roadster was a logical one. Except for a tonneau cover for the rain, there was no weather protection. The design plans from back then, however, include roof attachment points. Little thought was devoted to anything beyond necessities. The doors appear to have been cut into the flanks against their will, the thin handle can only be levered out of its wind-

41 ▪ 1
Whether on Austrian Alpine passes or in America's wide open spaces: Number One still embodies the ideals of happy, distraction-free driving

38 ▪ 1
The ignition lock was on the left, the tachometer was the sporting Porsche driver's only main instrument.

39 ▪ 1
Far from a do-it-yourself job, Number One was an amazingly mature vehicle with many refined details, and all the consistency of a mid-engined design.

cheating recess by applying counter-pressure. The headlights, flasher moldings, and bumpers possess the timeless beauty of what is truly functional. The same is true for the interior, which originally only boasted a tachometer dial – the speedometer was not added until later.

After switching on the ignition (you can hear the fuel pump ticking), you press a button to start – a neat way to become aware of the engine firing as a result of the fuel and spark elements coming together, something which has unfortunately been lost in today's world.

Sheet metal from the body shamelessly enters the cockpit. The border between inside and outside is only loosely symbolized by two glass panes that are set a flat angle, and offer only very limited protection against the wind. Two rubber lips push rain over the top edge of the glass onto the driver and passenger. Still, Number One was allowed a lockable glove compartment and map pockets on the leather-covered door trims. The brilliantly simple cable-pull handle, incidentally, was restored to life for the turn-of-the-century Audi TTS roadster.

Like most mid-engine vehicles, you can only reach the engine by lying on your stomach, and the conversions to peripherals and equipment repositioning that the engine required once it had been turned back-to-front were so extensive that there was hardly any trunk to speak of. This is why Porsche reverted to the rear-engine principle (and to a modified Volkswagen floor platform beneath a sheet-metal body).

Still, the unique path that Porsche began to pursue with the 356 goes back to this model, which was the first to set the signals once again for future success. And it's still astonishing: the more you look at Number One and understand it, the more you let the rear-end styling have its effect on you, along with the overall configuration, the closer you come to the origins of the current Boxster concept.

By the way: even back then, the ignition switch was on the left.

41·1

The Purist and His Roots

Encounters with Ferry Porsche

PORTRAIT

"THE BOSS IS COMING!" whispered the staff in the early morning as an elegant 356 drove through the gate. The announcment was made with both respect and admiration. It was the summer of 1959, and as a 20-year old, I had the first dream job of my life: trainee at Porsche, working in the Repair Department.

That is how I experienced Ferry Porsche back then. The ceremony was the same every day. Youthfully elegant and almost fragile in appearance, he would climb out of the coupe, walk across the lot, and make his way up the stairs to his office. His clothing was always sporty and correct, and had a certain British touch. He returned greetings from the employees in a friendly manner, and often exchanged a few words with the people who took on the repair jobs. So this was the man with the famous name! The man who, in the difficult days following the war, had turned a design office into a genuine small-scale automobile factory.
As a trainee, I was assigned to Mr. Brett, one of the legendary Repair

Department representatives who knew nearly every customer throughout the world. Mr. Brett got very enthusiastic when he spoke of the boss. "If you're ever concerned about something or have a problem, you can just go to the boss. He spares the time for you and really listens."

Nine years later, in September 1968, I had the first opportunity to find out for myself that Mr. Brett had been right. I was sitting with the boss – now Dr. Ferry Porsche – in the office. We were speaking about the possibility of my being given the position of Race Manager and PR Manager. Miss Werkmeister – back then we still said "Miss" – brought some coffee, and what was supposed to be a ten-minute formality turned into a long, profound conversation. As we began to philosophize about company goals and strategies, he made a key statement that I have never forgotten: "The most important thing is the continuity of the company. Everything else has to be subordinated to this goal, including the interests of the investors or the employees."

I liked that, and joined the team. At my first management meeting, one of the topics up for discussion was the balance sheet. The finance manager at that time wanted to increase the book value of the real assets, in other words the factory site and buildings. "After all," he said. "they're worth a fortune. Dr. Porsche didn't like that idea at all, and snubbed the finance manager: "In itself, this property isn't worth a thing. It is only worth something as long as we can produce and sell our cars. Who wants to buy an empty factory?"
What prophetic insight in a day of real estate speculation and general belief in the appreciation of land value! Porsche, who had been strongly influenced by the pre-war crisis, was later proven right – at the latest in the 1990's, when empty factories became obsolete and could be had for song.

The boss

So now Dr. Ferry Porsche was my boss too. I quickly found out for certain that Mr. Brett really had been right: The boss really did have time, and he took it. It became almost a ritual. Helene

44 ▪ 1

decisions. I can't say that I ever found that to be the case. What certainly was true, however, was that he did not often make rash decisions.

Every statement, every judgement was characterized by a profound knowledge of the branch and of contemporary history. The boss never saw the here and now as an isolated condition, but rather as the product of a development that began with the economic crisis at the end of 1920s, flowed uninterruptedly through the Third Reich to the catastrophe of the war and, after a difficult new start, emerged into the period of prosperity that had by the time I am speaking of here had lasted for quite a lengthy period.

This awareness of history can be illustrated very clearly with a small and yet somehow far from trivial episode that took place in Dr. Porsche's outer office. I walked in, took of my coat and hung it on a hanger in the wardrobe. Seeing this, Helene Werkmeister was horrified: "Oh, but you can't do it like that, Mr. Steinemann; the hook is facing in the wrong direction!" As I looked at her in utter astonishment, she added: "Of course, you wouldn't know that, since you're from Switzerland: If an air raid comes and you have to run down to the basement for shelter, every second is important. Putting the hook on in the wrong way gets you tangled up, and you lose three seconds!"

Werkmeister, the faithful soul from the outer office, used to say: "Go right on in, I'll bring some coffee."

Dr. Porsche received me in a cheerful and friendly manner, asked how I was doing and about my wife, and then wanted to hear about my concerns and the decisions that had to be made. His desk was always properly in order, but we rarely sat at it. Dr. Porsche preferred the club chairs and the smoker's table.

As I presented all my questions I soon realized that the boss could draw on a huge fund of experience from his days as engineer and test manager for the Porsche design office. He knew the company, the individual staff members, the suppliers, and the entire automotive industry. He weighed up decisions from all angles before he made them. Certain people back then used to say that the boss didn't like to make

44 ▪ 1

A picture taken on Ferry Porsche's 85th birthday: The professor at the wheel of Porsche Number 1

45 ▪ 1

The Porsche legend began in 1948 with Number 1: the 356 Roadster had a genuine mid- engine layout and was rated at 35 bhp, which – at an unladen weight of just 585 kg (1,290 lb) – was enough for 135 km/h (84 mph). To its left: the new 911 Cabriolet, latest model in a long development history

The Difference between Ferrari and Porsche

Two great marques, two great personalities, two worlds. A brief outline of the differences helps us to understand Ferry Porsche and the world of Zuffenhausen and Weissach better. In the late 1960s, the two marques had similar interests in their dealings with motor sport's FIA. This led to a dialogue in which I had to act as spokesman, since Enzo Ferrari spoke only Italian.

Ferrari, the lone wolf. The man who makes every decision all on his own. Who prefers a monolog to a dialog. Who dominates every conversation. Who is driven onward in motor sport by love, passion, and obsession. Who is not really an industrialist at all, but the manager of a racing team. Who only builds commercial cars so that the racing team can survive. Who wants to avoid cooperation and partnerships wherever possible.

Porsche, the conciliatory one. The man who makes decisions with others and delegates them as well. Who is open for dialog and can listen. Who races in order to put his cars in the spotlight (he also does it out of love, but with a certain degree of serenity). Who sees himself as an industrialist, and therefore as someone who is obligated to maintain production, jobs, and sales. Who is willing to cooperate and enter into partnerships. Two great men, two worlds.

In the workshops of Maranello and Weissach, however, these two worlds meet again: the same love of craftsmanship, the same professional pride, and the same respect for the boss influences all who work there.

"What if we built locomotives?"

Ferry Porsche was always a master of surprise, and often of disarming bonmots. Hardly one of these meetings over coffee ever went by without just such a rousing comment, that slipped out of him despite his otherwise very business-like approach to the subjects in hand. Nearly thirty years later, I still remember some of them.

The boss was known for his generosity to the emlpoyees; he favored a progressive style of leadership, and this was true for social issues as well. Every now and then, however, certain requests made in connection with overtime policy, for instance, went too far for him. In the middle of the conversation, he would say: "We've had this before. Back in the thirties during the Grossglockner Pass test drives: we stayed together after dinner and drank beer till after midnight. And then we charged those clever guys for it as overtime – after all, we had talked about cars!"
Constant wrangling over company cars and borrowing them for the evening or the weekend could also drive the boss up the wall when the demands got excessive. When he put his foot down, the message was clear: "What if we built locomotives here? Would you all still want to take one home with you at the weekend?"
Ferry Porsche did not place much trust in the banks, who treated the automotive industry in general (and Ferdinand Porsche in particular) very poorly in the late 1920s: "Those are institutions that rent umbrellas. And then when it starts to rain, they call all the umbrellas in."

46▪1

46▪1
The 928 GTS – a masterful sports tourer – was part of Professor Porsche's own fleet

47▪1
"Ferdinand" – the endearing nickname for the 356 prototype, which Ferdinand Porsche received as a gift for his 75th birthday from his son Ferry

Over the decades, Ferry Porsche also had some interesting experiences with his engineers. Budgeting development costs was not exactly their strength. I was totally perplexed as the boss explained his philosophy of development costs to me during one of these conversations: "My dear Steinemann, when an engineer comes in and says his development will cost us a million, than I calculate for myself one million multiplied by ten. This formula has always worked well for me."

Ferry Porsche was not always so jovial. On one occasion he was annoyed with me because I led to his losing his composure: It was just after the 1,000-kilometer race at the Nürburg Ring, on the Sunday afternoon; it had been a five-fold victory for Porsche. I ran to the telephone booth in the Sport Hotel and called the boss at his home on Feuerbacher Weg. In the booth next to me Franz-Josef Strauss, Bavaria's famed Prime Minister, was just ending a conversation. I beckoned him over and said: "Dr. Porsche, there is someone here who would like to congratualte you, let me pass you over to him." His reaction the next day: "You can't do that. If I had known that Franz-Josef Strauss was on the telephone, I would have stood up first!"

The farewell
Ferry Porsche and I left the stage of

48■1

active everyday business at almost the same time. The boss became Chairman of Porsche's Supervisory Board, and from then on guided its destiny by remote control.

The company continued to expand successfully, went public, and celebrated victories in innumerable races. There was also a multitude of national and international tributes of every kind, including the highest academic honors. But there were difficult times too. Ferry Porsche was deeply saddened by the death of his wife Dodo. And in later years, he had to experience the recession that he had always feared, which brought Porsche to the edge of ruin.

As the company celebrates its 50-year anniversary, it finds itself in a strong, vital, and future-oriented position. For me, this is cause to offer my hearty congratulations, but it also reminds me of a most eventful period of my life, with a great boss.
For me, THE BEST!

Biographical information

1909   Birth of Ferdinand Porsche, known as "Ferry," on September 19th in Wiener Neusatdt, Austria. School in Wiener Neustadt and in Stuttgart/ Bad Cannstatt, Germany. Technical training in Stuttgart at Bosch.

1931   Designer in the development office run by his father, Dr. Ing. h.c. Ferdinand Porsche, in Stuttgart.

1932   Added responsibilities include traffic monitoring and coordination, and also participation in the design and development of the Auto Union Grand Prix racing car.

1934   Test-drive manager for the "Volkswagen".

1935   Marriage to Dorothea Reitz from Stuttgart (who died in 1985). They had four sons.

1938   Manager of the Testing Department. The design office moved to the new building in Zuffenhausen.

1940   Assistent managing director of the company.

1945   Managing director of the company, which moved to Gmünd in Carinthia (Austria) during the war. Start of development work on the legendary Porsche 356 based on the Volkswagen; the first car to bear the Porsche name.

1949   After the first 46 Type 356 cars had been built in Gmünd, return with the company to Stuttgart-Zuffenhausen, together with the principal members of the staff. Re-establish-

48■1
The fascination of the 911 Turbo began in 1975

ment of the consulting engineers' office for contract development work.

1950   Start of Porsche 356 series production in Stuttgart.

1959   Award of the Grand Cross for Distinguished Service by the President of the Federal Republic of Germany, Professor Theodor Heuss.

1965   Award of the title "Dr. techn. E.h." by the Vienna Institute of Technology.

1972   Chairman of the Board of Management of Dr. Ing. h.c. F. Porsche KG, after the company went public.

1975   Award of the "Grand Golden Badge of Honor" of the Republic of Austria in Vienna.

1978   Award of the Wilhelm Exner Medal to Dr. Ferdinand Porsche.

1979   Award of the Federal Republic of Germany's Star to the Grand Cross for Distinguished Service on the occasion of his 70th birthday.

1981   Award of the Gold Medal of the "Société de l'Automobile." Honorary citizenship of the town of Zell am See, Austria.

1984   Award of the title "Professor" by Prime Minister Späth of the German State of Baden-Wuerttemberg.

1985   Appointment as "Senator E.h." of the University of Stuttgart.

1989   Award of the Economic Medal for outstanding service to the economy of the State of Baden-Wuerttemberg by Minister for the Economy Herzog.

1989   Award of the City of Stuttgart's Citizen's Medal on December 12, on the occassion of his 80th birthday, in honor of his outstanding contribution to the ecomomic development of the state capital.

1990   Honorary chairmanship of the Supervisory Board (from 1993 on, honorary chairmanship without mandate)

1994   Award of honorary citizenship of the town of Wiener Neustadt.

CHAPTER 3

Lightweight success

The 550/RS60 and Porsche 904 racing machines, the Boxster as the bearer of Porsche's streamlined heritage – here we see the taut lines drawn across the years, characterized by a no-compromise attitude, top engineering skill, and unswerving passion for motor sport. Again and again, the pure Porsche virtues shine through: Lightweight construction. Torsion-resistant frames. Low center of gravity. Technologically avant-garde in their conception, design, and choice of materials. Nevertheless, thought its sounds like a harmonious recipe, in practice, it always proved to harbor an assortment of problems, which had to be removed one little piece at a time with great persistence, until the pure, fully matured car emerged: a Porsche!

550/RS 60
The hammering of the early years

BOXSTER
Room for two golf bags, (with an engine in between) – no one can accuse Porsche of not taking the desires of the market into consideration

904
Hot rod – made of plastic

Pure Porsche:
The Roadster with Punch

by David Staretz

52 ■ 1

THE RUST-COLORED surface of Marble Canyon Road was covered with pale morning light that looked like flax draped over the sharp crests of the rock ridges. The moon hung in the sky like a knife that the night had left behind.

It was six o'clock in the morning and minus 23 degrees Fahrenheit (5 degrees Celsius) in Arizona. It was hopelessly cold. The engine, with its shaft-driven overhead camshafts, was not in a particularly good mood, and had to be regularly stimulated by rythmically pressing the gas pedal. The wide open spaces were, as ever, crisp and clear as the car floated across the desert floor. The fever that had arrived in the night lent dramatic intensity to the environment: you could see how the stage might have been set for a death in Hollywood.

Somebody had lent me a splendidly wide cowboy coat, but I put more trust in my Corsican cap, made of black felt, stiffened by the rain, crushed out of shape by use. I pulled it down ridiculously low over my ears – my own kind of soft top.

The oil-pressure gauge needle vibrated slightly and gave me the go-ahead; with a shake, I felt the car overcome its coughing, bone-dry displeasure – for too long it had dragged along behind the camera car at a mere 30 km/h, but now it was relieved as the tachometer reached the 4,000 rpm mark and continued to climb. I pressed down my elbows as well as I could, clung to the steering wheel at the twenty after seven position, and tried to slip down even deeper into the seat – the Porsche's cold-rivetted windshield lifted the direct wind flow up over my head, but it poured back down onto my neck as a cold wave and swirled around in the car's interior from behind. The mid-engine located behind my back was indeed

52 ■ 2

52 ■ 3

52 ■ 4

550/RS 60

52 ■ 1-4/53 ■ 1

Getting up early in Arizona. Here, Porsche driving takes on a dimension that quickly makes it clear why these cars were always so successful in America: they are the perfect contrast to the landscape

55 ■ 1

55 ■ 2

55 ■ 1

In the early light: The 550 is an example of pure theory: light, agile, direct. An uncomplicated everyday roadster for weekend victories

55 ■ 2

Silver Bullet: The 550 Spyder gave the facination of pure metal a new aspect – sensual, but air-dryed

54 ■ 1

The big Fuhrmann: 160 bhp from 1,600 cubic centimeters – the RS 60 had an ingenious power plant that walked the tightrope between genious and madness, but was amazingly well suited for long distances

close, and as loud as expected, but it didn't offer any warmth.

Mid engines have a long tradition at Porsche – even the legendary Number One had the Volkswagen "boxer" flat-four behind the seats, just in front of the rear axle. Something to remember: If a company builds mid-engine cars, you can be sure that the engineers have the last word.

By 1953, six years later, the financial situation had improved enough to start the first big sports-car project: production of the 550 model (no longer in the Carinthian town of Gmünd, but in Zuffenhausen, Germany). It was introduced at the Paris Motor Show. What the visitors saw was a small, light, sporty two-seater that had been hammered out of aluminum; it was obviously aerodynamic, and had no roof.

A no-compromise car, designed for the sole purpose of winning races – primarily street races, but also long-distance classics, such as Le Mans and the Nürburg Ring, where there were the appropriate engine-size categories.

For the record: the official 550 was preceded by a series of remarkable cars made by Walter Glöckler, a car dealer from Frankfurt. Together with a Porsche engineer, Glöckler had coaxed the 1100 cc Volkswagen engine up to 58 bhp, turned it around, installed it backwards in a tubular space frame and – it seems that people had a feeling for beauty back then – had an attractive aluminum body panel-beaten over it. After initial racing success, Glöckler also had access to the 90–bhp engine. His work thus paved the way for the Porsche 550 designed by engineer Wilhelm Hild. For beauty's sake, the same company that did Glöckler's car was asked to do the body: Weidenhausen in Frankfurt.

Another thing to keep in mind is that, back then, Porsches did not have the same kind of production-model character as today's production cars – numerous versions and body modifications were derived from the basic model; in dur

56 ▪ 1

course, the line was expanded to include the sensational Fuhrmann engine. This highly sophisticated racing unit with four camshafts enjoyed immediate success.

The 550's very first race (in its first year, the car was not yet known as the Spyder) were run with the tuned 1500 Super, a direct offshoot of the Volkswagen engine. With a compression ratio of 12.5 : 1, this alcohol-fueled power plant produced a bold 100 PS. Despite carburetor problems, this was enough to enable driver Helm Glöckler (a cousin) to secure the first victory with the 550, a car that would later be crowned with innumerable successes. (In the Le Mans 24–hour race, the two teams Richard von Frankenberg/Paul Frère and Hans Herrmann/Helm Glöckler won a masterful double victory in their class.)

The Fuhrmann engine, also known as the 547 or Carrera engine, was not put into the hands of private drivers until 1954, since it first had to be rendered a whole lot more unburstable.

A distinction was made between the VW-based push-rod engines (with the camshaft in the block), identifiable by model names such as 356 A, B, C or Super 90, and the double overhead-camshaft engine that was fit for racing and heroically earned such names as the Panamericana Spyder, 356 Carrera, Mille Miglia Spyder, and later, the James Dean Spyder.

Dean had a customer version suitable for car racing, taken from a small contingent of 550 RS models (RS stands for *Rennsport*, the German word for racing); it had been delivered to the active West Coast importer, John Neumann. Dean had to pay what was then nearly 25,000 German marks for his "Little Bastard" – though he did not have to fork out the whole sum in cash, since his Porsche Speedster was taken as a trade in.

This legendary car – which became unstoppable on the road to Cholame on the afternoon of September 30, 1955 – gave Porsche a bigger-than-life dimension, so strong that people were able to multiply it through the use of any given hysteria-factor. In a certain sense, there was a positive aspect to the tragedy: imagine the situation if J.D.'s accident had been in a Humber!

A year later, it was Umberto Maglioli who celebrated the 550 Spyder's most spectacular racing success: Driving alone, he defeated his Goliath-size competitors in the Targa Florio. After ten 72-kilometer laps through the mountains of Cerda in stifling heat, this Piedmont driver won the race by a margin of 15 minutes. That was the most important, and the most gratifying, sporting success that the Porsche company had enjoyed up until then.

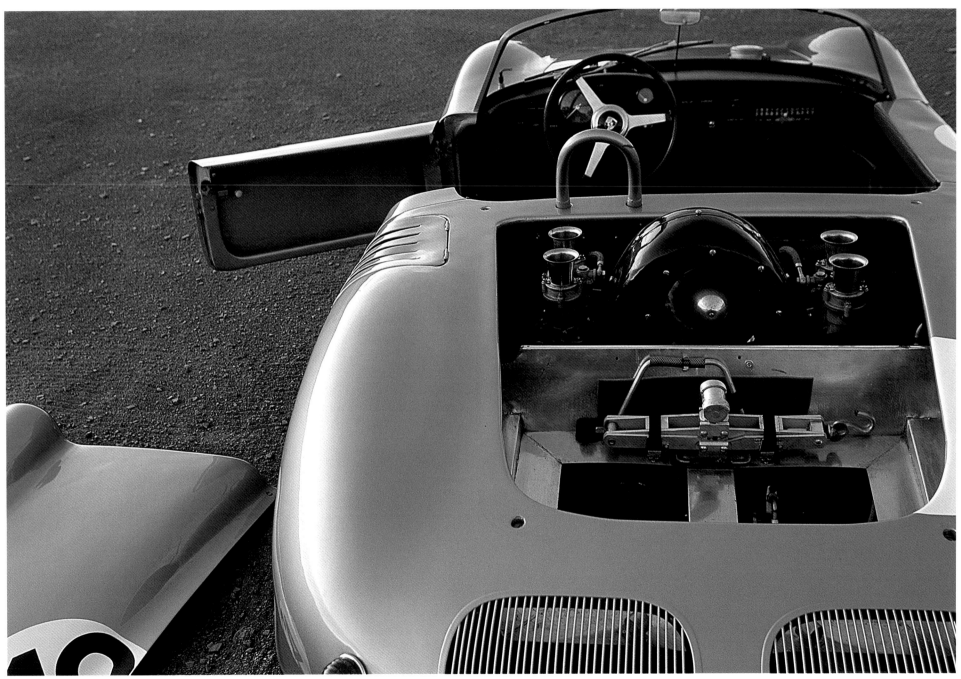

The Fuhrmann engine was a technological treat: its block was cast in light alloy; the four cylinders and their heads were also made of aluminum. Right from the beginning of production, the engine turned 110 and 117 bhp out of 1,498 cc, whereby the camshafts were not driven by a chain, but by two vertical shafts. The cylinders were filled by two Solex 40PJJ dual-barrel downdraft carburetors. The engine had two ignition coils, two distributors, and two spark plugs per cylinder. This made for sensational results: the engine ran up to 7,800 rpm in order to reach its peak power output.Since it weighed just 594 kilograms, the car could boast a top speed of up to 235 km/h, a fact which shows that it was possible to achieve good aerodynamics with a good eye. The aluminum body, which was hammered over a simple ladder-type tubular frame, featured parts of the chassis and suspension from the series-production 356 – which explains why it took only four months to develop the car.

Yet what was really great about the Spyder's lightweight construction (and still is today) is its freedom from a different kind of weight – the weight of tradition. And so this loud, incompatible, gleaming piece of silver cuts through the desert of Arizona. The sky has turned blue in the heat. Right below you, the completely empty, rust-colored Highway 89 heads for the mountains like an angry brahman bull. In the mid-day heat, you can hear the wheels working; slight imbalances work their way in periodically; each speed has its own sound in this unfiltered sensation.

Hard clutch. Notchy shift. Not much play in the steering. This car is the here and now. Every part can be understood mechanically: welding, screwing, turning, folding, pressing – the gamut of hot and cold metal processing, the result of ingenious calculation. And yet there is so much breath in the cold metal, so much bestial life, filled with this impetuous, hammering desire for ascintillating surge of power. Light, flat, agile; with this sports chassis and suspension (still ideal to-

day), the close gear ratios, the sharp brakes ready to pounce, the lively steering reactions. Here, removed from time and space, the little car trumpets its qualities into the canyon with audacity and pleasure – pure beauty in its element. It is fully at home in the speed that shapes itself around the body like the expression of immortality with which such moments can be measured.

A bare heart in the midst of naked technology – up to your neck in bare metal. Spartan equipment, single-syllable feelings – as a time machine, the Spyder makes clear what an unbelievably fleet-footed automobile it must have been in the 1950's, how well the 117 bhp got along with the alloy body, what an elegant solution the mid-engine design was and is.

The 550's layout served as an ideal starting point: for further competition developments, but also for sales to customers, which now began to be worthwhile.

✳

Nevertheless, what appears to be the "grandfather of the Boxster" is a pure-bred racing machine: from the RS 60 Spyder, it was just one, admittedly complex, step to Porsche's Formula 1 efforts in the early 1960's, which saw little success. Outstanding results were still being achieved, however, in all kinds of long-distance races. Success was also found in Formula 2, with different 550 deviants known as RSK's (the K stood for the shape of a new type of front-wheel geometry) or with the 718/1500 Spyder, an evolved model.

The decision was made to orient the company more strongly toward the sports car segment again, particularly since new sports car rules were established in 1960.

The key elements were a higher windshield, a hinged engine hood, and something resembling a trunk. In accordance with this, Porsche changed the RSK into a 718 RS 60, which was later modified to become the 718/8 RS Spyder, and was

61 ■ 1
Erratic casting:
The body appears to have set solid in the driving wind like thick liquid heat poured over the wheels

59 ■ 1
Extreme in the middle:
Those who design mid-engine cars have a weakness for problems. One of these was engine access, another was the cooling. Nevertheless, the advantage of ideal weight distribution is undeniable

58 ■ 1
The beautiful:
The engine thumped unevenly in the cool air like a shadow boxer-losing his rhythm at the sight of an attractive woman

then powered by the air-cooled, eight-cylinder "boxer" engine that had in the meantime been designed for Formula 1. As a two-liter unit, it produced 210 bhp, which made for a top speed of 260 km/h and for great success in long-distance racing: Targa Florio, Nürburg Ring, numerous victories in the USA, impregnable dominance in the European Hillclimb Championship.

Our RS 60 still had the souped-up "four-cylinder Fuhrmann," which was now a 1,600 unit rated at 160 bhp, and was good for numerous long-distance successes: overall victory in the 44th Targa Florio, for instance, with Herrmann/Bonnier finishing ahead of Ferrari and linking up with the Targa triumphs of 1956 and 1959. In its first entry in the Sebring 12-hour race, Oliver Gendebien and Hans Herrmann won ahead of Holbert and Scheckter, who made up the second RS 60 works team.

Panting. Wheezing. A victim of its own high-strung nature – a calm attempt to control the breathing using the gas pedal makes one thing clear: A hyperventilating artist is suffering from attacks between genius and madness, burning all ends of the candle of its existence, approximately four. Finally the tense power unit seems to calm itself, it feels that I know its fever, and senses the direction in which I am leading it in with whispering patience: Forwards! Gasping, with a runny nose and a few tentative flourishes, it clears out its coughing fit, gains in volume, begins to hammer, to roar, and to sound off, then becomes soft and supple like the sensuous curves that rise above the wheels. The slim steering wheel picks up and conveys vibrations that come from the road. Nothing remains veiled for this suspension and chassis. Forces penetrate through the pivot points like vector arrows. They seek you out in your small leather bucket seat – a seat in which Jochen Mass recently suffered for 2,000 kilometers in order to win the Targa Tasmania, one of the most-reputable long-distance races for historic cars. I bet that he had a lot of fun; this car is a thoroughbred at the peak of its maturity.

The engine now rejoices its way up and over the 6,000 rev mark, and the deep-red rocks reflect back the sound so well that you begin to worry about acoustic feedback.

Petite, reduced to the maximum, and with plenty of punch, this *Silver Bullet* flows through the mountains. Like a shot fired in revenge, it can be heard from a long way away. Almost centered in the cockpit (too far from the armrests) you are totally surrendered to the seat, dedicated to the steering – a shock absorber in the midst of vibrating sheet metal. The tachometer seems to have flipped as the needle swings to the eight mark at the very top – one functional detail among many. The pedal layout (which makes it possible to brake and double declutch with the ball of your foot and your heel) is another example. With the plain stick shift, you put the engine down into third (the best music). When the hindquarters become light, the car – coolly in charge in its own territory (the boundary region) – sweeps over the surface, which has turned the color of poisonous lead oxide. Up front you can see the white truck with the open garage door that leads directly back to the museum. One last touch of the pedal, and a backfire shatters through the canyon like the crack of doom.

THE PORSCHE LEGEND IN THE USA

by David Staretz

992

63 ▪ 1

The Boxster's instrument layout clearly echoes that of the 550 Spyder: tachometer in the middle, temperature display on the right, speedometer on the left

64/65

There has seldom been a car with as many agreeable features as the Boxster has. Even the wind whirls softly past. It just loves the car's smooth underbody – which alone accounts for six percent of the reduction in aerodynamic drag

63 ▪ 1

THE ESSENCE OF PORSCHE is set free under the sun in the Boxster. Driving it offers the most clear and direct explanation: supple and vibrationless, undisturbed by troublesome turbulence, always alert, always agile around the central pivotal point where the engine is located.

No other sports car configuration influences driving in practice as positively as a "boxer" or horizontally opposed power unit, installed in the middle of the car with the transmission flanged directly to it, dragging the center of gravity right into the focal point, as it were.

Having chosen this layout, space was created for two extensive load areas (one at the front, one at the rear). In the middle, there is ample space for the car's occupants to sit and worry if they do not happen to own the two golf bags that the Porsche designers spared no effort to make possible.

At first, the fact that the Boxster has become a miracle of empty space may irritate Porsche lovers of dense, concentrated substance, but if examined more closely, it becomes easier to understand the technological aspects. Thanks to the mid-engine, there are so many other crucial advantages, such as the low moment of inertia around the vertical axis, which means that our Boxster goes around corners like an Indian temple dancer moves: always pivoting gracefully around the middle, always in perfect balance.

There was also space for a flat, elongated and correspondingly relaxed chassis and suspension layout, with aluminum longitudinal and transverse control arms and McPherson struts (optimized by Porsche, as its engineers like to

add). No yaw, no corrective movements at the end of the curve – cornering is always notable for the Boxster's good-natured acceptance of the limits as they approach; it tends towards understeer, slows itself down providing that no intentional load reversal takes place at the rear wheels (for instance, by engaging the clutch sharply or – in the case of the Tiptronic shift – giving the gas pedal a hefty push). In such cases, however, 204 horsepower can become the determining factor when each of them has only 6.13 kilograms to move.

The fact that the Porsche Boxster, a hedonistic fun machine, is defined here in terms of technology makes perfect sense, since it is precisely cars bearing the Porsche name that teach us so clearly that technology can harbor all kinds of sensuality and poetry (right up to transfiguration).

The most famous example of this is the famous 550 Speedster purchased by James Byron Dean, a twenty-four year old actor, who – at the intersection of Routes 46 and 41, just short of a mile south of Cholame, a small California town – was involved in the most famous car accident in history.

This fatal, yet essentially banal, meeting of man and machine snowballed into an unstoppable cult, which – with a healthy dose of American-style hype – went far beyond any measure of reason. There was no shortage of conspiracy, suicide or survival theories: James Dean was killed by the CIA, James Dean couldn't make it with Pier Angeli because in any case he was homosexual, James Dean lives, but is so

66■1

66■2

66■3

66■4

66 ▪ 1-4

Look at it from any angle – the Boxster is surely best of all when seen from the rear. Here we find evidence of the old, thrifty vocabulary of uncommunicative engineers – even if it is true that there was too much talk about a single golf bag. But driving along the old Route 66 revealed the following: This car loves America, and it loves women too, and proves it, for instance, by not tussling their hair – thanks to its ingenious ways of suppressing turbulence on the move. It is often such considerations that account for the difference between success and failure

horribly disfigured that no one is able to recognize him. When every detail of an incident is raised to a level far larger than life, true mystification makes its presence felt. Even tough Americans, such as the well-known car customizer George Barris, to whom Dean gave the task of enhancing the appearance of his 550 Spyder (including the *"Little Bastard" badge*), suddenly appeared in public with a ghastly message, as English author Stephen Bailey reports in an essay:

"Barris remembers: 'There was something strange about this car … a feeling, bad vibrations, an aura. Call it what you want … it got to me. Dean was all hyped up about it, and how he was going to drive it in the race, but I couldn't get excited about the car … I had a strange feeling about the whole thing and didn't want to let him drive away.'

A disastrous chain of ominous events related to the wreck turned the down-to-earth body-shop owner into a believer in the supernatural: Barris had purchased the wreck for 2,500 dollars with the intention of taking it apart and selling all the useable parts. A mechanic broke both legs when the wreck slid off the truck; a Beverly Hills doctor who had purchased the engine, was killed with it, and another racing doctor who installed the transmission in his car, was seriously injured when the car flipped over; in the end, the wreck was paradoxically sent on a tour by the Greater Los Angeles Safety Council, labeled with instructive statements such as: 'This

accident could have been prevented.' During one of these appearances, in Sacramento, the wreck fell off its steel frame and broke the hip of a teenager. At a later exhibition in 1959, in New Orleans, it broke apart into several pieces."

The fact that a celebrated car owned by a celebrated actor should ber pursued by such macaber stories should not worry us – the tension exerted by deep-drawn sheet metal is often enormous. Often enough it is precicely in this area – where technology manifests itself through precision and incorruptability – that the source of all that is magical and unpredictable seems to lie.

We have all found ourselves in situations like this, for instance when we have borrowed a fountain pen that has been broken in by someone else, ridden a motorcycle through a winter night, or coaxed a computer through difficulties both before and after program crashes.

The peculiarities and entrophies of technology are the determining factors, which make it fascinating – not least because it can culminate in unavoidable catastrophes. Any attempt we make to grasp these things proves again just how inaccessible technology is. It is precisely here that the fascination lies, and this can still be seen best when we consider the automobile, a highly concentrated form of technology in immediate proximity to our lives.

A Car that's a Shooting Star Even at a Standstill

by Helmut Zwickl

904

69.1

68.1

The Porsche 904 Carrera GTS Coupé was one of the most successful sports cars of the 1960s

69.1

The 904 anticipated much of the technology that would be later become standard in racingcars: mixed steel/plastic construction, low weight and frontal area

YOU SIT AT EYE LEVEL with passing German Shepherd dogs, but when the traffic light switches to green, you have no opposition.

Nor did those who drove the car in the two-liter GT category have much opposition in 1964 and 1965. And it was actually possible to drive the 904 Carrera GTS, this purest of all sports instruments, on public roads as well.

This coupé, a car about as high as an ironing board, a car that never saw the inside of a wind tunnel, joins the ranks of timeless sport car sculptures.

In this glorious brush stroke from the hand of Ferdinand Alexander "Butzi" Porsche is speed in plastic form. Even at a standstill the 904 is a shooting star.

The 904 made optimum use of the FIA's GT rules for the 1964 motorsport season: 100 of these cars had to be produced for homologation, which was no trouble at all for Porsche. A potent group of waiting customers snatched this piece of machinery, which cost 29,700 German marks, out of the Zuffenhausen manufacturer's hands. Not only was the car suitable for racing circuits and hillclimbs, it had also been toughened up on the VW proving ground for long-distance races and rallies. Back then, no other racing-car company subjected itself to endurance tests of this kind.

The new flat six "boxer" engine was not available in time for the 904, so the first 104 cars were powered by the tried-and-tested four-cylinder, four-camshaft engine from the Carrera 2, which left a lot of unused space in the tail. The engine

was the only thing that had already been tried out in advance. Know-how for the suspension had been gained in Formula 1; everything else in this car was an expedition into unknown territory for Porsche.

There was an unexpected departure from a tubular space frame in favor of a box-type frame with a plastic body.

The logic behind this decision was this: for a tubular frame, only a light-alloy body could be considered, and the expenditure for tools, welding, fastening, and modelling of the body would have been too high for the number of cars to be produced. At first, the sheet-metal box-type frame with two side rails and cross elements proved to be less torsionally resistent than the tubular frame, and it was not until the plastic body was bonded and screwed on that the rigidity was doubled.

The cockpit cell was particularly rigid; the bucket seats were molded into the structure, and there was no seat adjustment. Instead, the drivers had to have the pedal positions modified and adjust the telescopic steering column.

Problems with the first prototype, which began its test program in August 1963, ranged from loose adhesive bonds and the wheels cutting into the fenders, to fractured trailing arms, broken engine mounts and front brake temperatures that were much too high, not to mention the fact that the front of the car began to lift at 180 km/h (112 mph).

In light of this avalanche of problems which bore down on Porsche's engineers, the level of refinement the car reached in such a short time is astonishing.

71 ■ 1

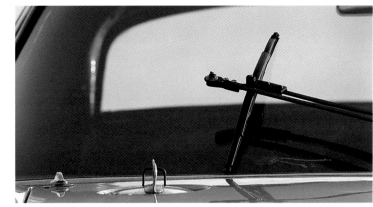

71 ■ 2

70 ■ 1 - 71 ■ 3

*This was the first Porsche with a
plastic body, a principle that
caused problems at first:
Adhesive bonds separated, the air
bubbles in the Palatal plastic were
gradually eliminated (but not some
time had elapsed); nevertheless,
the Type 904 reached a high level
of technical refinement within
a short period.*

*The fact that it is still considered
to be one of the most attractively
styled sports cars of all time,
somehow seems almost secondary*

71 ■ 3

The bodies – made at the Heinkel aircraft factory in from BASF Palatal plastic by an injection process – lost up to 50 kg (110 lb) during the course of production. There too, a learning process had to be undertaken, since final curing of the fiber-glass reinforced plastic and cutting of the plastic parts proved to present difficulties.

Air pockets were eliminated at 75° C (167° F) in the drying oven. With 80 workers, it was possible to complete two bodies per day at the Heinkel factory.

For the customers, the 904 was supplied with a street exhaust and a racing exhaust system. With 180 bhp on tap at 7,200 rpm, the factory quoted a top speed of 263 km/h (163 mph). The "street" exhaust tamed the engine down to 155 bhp at 6,900 rpm and a top speed of 250 km/h (155 mph). For a two-liter car weighing just 650 kg (1,433 lb), these values were unrivaled. Only the two-liter Abarth, which was not a mid-engined but a rear-engined car, was close to competing with the 904; yet it could only do this in the dragster discipline, in other words in a straight line. As far as roadholding, handling, and stability are concerned, the 904 was a milestone development, as it was soon able to prove with a double victory in the 1964 Targa Florio.

Colin Davis/Baron Pucci finished twelve minutes ahead of Herbert Linge/Gianni Balzarini. The 904 four-cylinder was unbeatable on the mountainous course; Ferrari did not start due to a works decision; and of the five 4.7-liter Cobras that Caroll Shelby entered, only one survived.

Something to keep in mind: in this Targa, a 904 Coupé with the eight-cylinder engine also lined up at the start, driven by Maglioli/Barth.

A 904 could take a deep breath and dispose of a standing kilometer (0.62 mile) in 24.5 seconds. Even today it can catapult you from a standstill to 100 km/h (62 mph) – in a car now treated as a priceless classic – in six seconds; after 11.8 seconds it is moving at 160 km/h (99 mph). Being inside a cello could hardly feel much different than being in the 904 cockpit, where the engine resonances are unnaturally amplified and assail your ear drums with a veritable acoustic feast.

The 904 was a big hit with private drivers. The factory even considered building a second 100-unit series for 1965. But even in those days Ferdinand Piëch, who in the meantime had become head of the testing department, was no friend of stagnation. For 1965 the 904 was made a bit stronger and more rigid at critical points; 20 more 904s were built for prototype use with the six and eight cylinder engines before Piëch launched the 906 (better known as the Carrera-6) in 1966. It again had a tubular frame, and unlike the 904 was not a compromise, but a truly leading-edge design that complied with the sports car rules, which prescribed 50 cars for homologation.

But the 904 was surely the more beautiful car.

72 ▪ 1
This is how competitors usually saw it! Some of the 904's most significant successes were the double victory in the Targa Florio, and first places in the Tour de France,the 1,000-kilometer (622 mile) race on the Nürburg Ring, and the Le Mans 24-hour race

CHAPTER 4

The Icon

Few products radiate so much personality that they become a company's true trademark. The Porsche 911 is one of the exceptions. With its formal language and technical authority, the 911 defines the essence of a Porsche.

In the first 34 years of a story that seems to have no end, the Porsche 911 questioned the limits of its growth again and again. In the search for eternal youth, the 911 forged ahead tirelessly with new strength. When its career began in 1964, a displacement of two liters and an output of 130 bhp seemed a valid measure of all things on the German "autobahn". Today, the visible limit is represented by a Turbo with a 3.6-liter engine developing something in excess of 430 horsepower. And the next 911 generation has appeared on the horizon, to take the car into the next millennium with more performance than ever at its disposal.

TYPES
34 annual 911 vintages, each of them a further step towards perfection

TECHNO 959
A monument to the technically feasible: in 1985, the Porsche 959 was well ahead of its time

911 SAFARI
A Porsche goes hunting for big game

IMMUTABLE
Porsche for life: test driver, Herbert Linge

by Jürgen Lewandowski
Drawings by Serge Bellu

Trademarks and Icons

35 years are enough to make the 911 a legend

IN THE MID-FIFTIES, FERRY PORSCHE was already thinking about how and in what form a successor for the 356 could materialize. In the midst of all the ideas, one thing was clear: the new one would also be a coupe.

"We were living in an attractive niche," Ferry Porsche remembered later, "and with a sedan, we would have had to face up tothe giants – and we would probably have lost that game."

was always clear that the succesor would have to be a fastback too, in order to demonstrate its relationship with the 356," he later said about the **901**, as the car celebrated its world premiere in September 1963 at the Frankfurt Motor Show. The fact that the 901 became the 911 was due to a court order obtained by the Peugeot company, which in the Fall of 1964 succeeded in asserting its right to all three-digit

possible increases in the displacement later. No-one anticipated in November 1960 – as the engine began to run on the testing rig with an output of 120 brake horsepower – that it would eventually reach 3.8 liters.

When the **911** was delivered to its first customers at the end of 1964, the air-cooled horizontally opposed "boxer" engine has a displacement of 1991 cc

911 MODELS

76∎1

76∎2

76∎3

By the end of October 1959, the concept for the 356's successor had crystallized: With a wheelbase extended by 10 cm (3.9 inches) to 2.20 meters (86.6 inches) the interior space that people had been demanding for a long time was finally available. Moreover Ferdinand Alexander "Butzi" Porsche – appointed by his father as Chief of Design – created an exciting form: "It

model designations with a number with "0" in the middle.

For Ferry Porsche, it was clear early on that the classic four-cylinder engine would soon reach the end of its carreer – a displacement of much more than two liters was impracticable. So work was begun on a six-cylinder engine that would start life with a displacement of two liters, but would offer reserves for

and developed exactly 130 bhp at 6,100 rpm. That over the years this power unit would prove suitable for ever-increasing performance was due largely to the fact that Ferry Porsche gave way to the demands of his engineers (one of whom was Ferdinand Piëch, who worked in Stuttgart during the summer breaks until his studies at the ETH in Zurich were complete and

76∎1

The 911 set off on its triumphal march with just 130 bhp on tap

76∎2

In 1967, the Targa replaced the forgotten Cabriolet

76∎3

The first 911 S featured a 160 bhp engine and aluminium wheels

was permanently employed from April 1964 on). From dry sump lubrication to the best possible materials, he and they gave the six-cylinder power unit everything it needed to be something special right from the start.

The 911 was first offered for sale as a

Launched in 1967, the **Targa** appealed to buyers who like to drive with the roof open. Porsche also had a genuine convertible planned at first, but they soon realized that – as noted in a report – "a convertible version had not been taken into account when designing the

the **911 S**, came the first of many stages of evolution; at 6,600 rpm the uprated engine produced a respectable 160 bhp from the unchanged swept volume of 1991 cc. At 225 km/h (140 mph), the 911 S fulfilled the desire for more speed, and as well as the

77■1

77■2

77■3

coupe with a price tag of 23,900 German Marks, which made the new car about 7,000 German marks more expensive than the 356 C, which remained in the model line until 1965.

The 911 did indeed offer more interior space and comfort than the 356 C, but cars in this price class were rarities. For this reason, a decision was made on June 15, 1964, to offer the 901 (as it was still called at the time) with a four-cylinder engine, as the 902. This model came out in 1966 as the 912 with the reworked, 90-horsepower four-cylinder engine from the Porsche 356.

The decision to make the 912 turned out to be an inspired one, since there were a lot of customers who liked the shape of the 911, but did not want all that power – in the end 27,738 912 coupes and 2,562 Targas were built.

coupe, which meant that changes to the doors, door windows, and rear lid would be required, which would make a convertible very expensive."

Instead of this, Ferdinand Alexander Porsche created a massive roll bar, with a removable roof panel extending up to the windshield and a rear window made of plastic which could be removed by opening a zipper. Der Targa – the name was derived from the Sicilian Targa Florio road race, which Porsche won for the first time in 1956 with Umberto Maglioli at the wheel of a 550 A Spyder – was available as a 911 or a 912. And it lived up to all expectations: over the years, nearly one third of the all 911s were Targas.

Very soon, there was a cry for more power, and so in 1967, in the form of

wider rear fenders, had another new feature soon to become very popular: forged aluminum wheels from the Fuchs company.

The two-liter engine was developed further as the years went by. In 1968, for example the 911 T (with 110 bhp), the 911 L (with 130 bhp), and the unchanged 911 S (with 160 bhp) were all in the model line. For more comfort , one could choose the semi-automatic transmission with a torque converter and four gears. A year later, Porsche adopted mechanical fuel injection on the 911 E (140 bhp) and 911 S (170 bhp). In 1969 the wheelbase was lengthened from 2,211 to 2,268 millimeters (87 to 89.3 inches), for gains in interior space and driving stability. The Targa became available with a fixed glass rear window at about this time.

77■1
The least powerful of all 911s: the 911 T with 110 bhp engine

77■2
With fuel injection: the 911 E , with 165 bhp engine, arrived in 1972

77■3
Its "duck's tail" made it famous: the Carrera RS

The new decade saw the first increase in the 911's displacement – from 1970 on, dealers were able to offer cars with a 2195 cc engine. This was the year in duction in the compression ratio, so that the engines could now be run on regular gasoline with a lower octane number. The result was a 911 T with 215/60 VR 15 tires (the widest produced at that time) on 7-inch rims.

Sine the Carrera RS was designed for

78■1

78■2

78■3

which production of the 912 ceased. The new basic version of Porsche's coupé still bore the designation 911 T, but now produced 125 bhp at 5,800 rpm, while the 911 E developed 155 bhp at 6,200 rpm. It would seem, however, that the power-hungry people interested in Porsches mostly dreamed about the 911 S, which, at 6,500 rpm, developed 180 bhp, enough to accelerate the car to 225 km/h (140 mph). To keep this kind of performance under control when slowing down as well, all cars from this model year on were equipped with ventilated disc brakes as standard equipment.

At the beginning of the 1970s – particularly in the USA – exhaust emission laws became increasing strict. Porsche responded to this challenge with a further increase in engine displacement. For the 1972 season, the 911 entered the market with a 2341 cc engine; this increase went hand in hand with a re-

130 bhp at 5,600 rpm and a top speed of 205 km/h (127 mph), a **911 E** with 165 bhp at 6,200 rpm and 220 km/h (136 mph), and – again uprated – the 911 S with 190 bhp at 6,500 rpm and 230 km/h (143 mph).

Nevertheless, the sensation of the model year was the **911 Carrera RS**, with its rear spoiler that would enter history as the "duck's tail." The extremely fast Carrera RS – good for 245 km/h (152 mph) – was developed in order for Porsche to have a basic model suitable for racing. The six-cylinder engine now had a swept volume of 2687 cc, and at 6,300 rpm produced a sensational 210 bhp. The Carrera RS was a remarable car in many ways. It was the first Porsche, for instance, to have tires of different dimensions: up front there were 185/70 VR 15 tires mounted on 6-inch wide rims, while at the rear, it was shod with

motor sport, Ferry Porsche hoped to find the 500 buyers needed for type approval of the car during 1972. As it turned out, the Porsche community had just been waiting for 210 bhp at a price of 34,000 German Marks – in the end, no less than 1,580 of these models (including the 55 pure-bred **911 RSR** racing cars) rolled off the production line. Of these 1,308 were ordeedr with the more luxurious touring package, which matched the 911 S's equipment and trim. The remainder were lightweight versions tipping the scales at about 100 km (220 lb) less than the Touring RS, which weighed 1,075 kg (2,370 lb). It is easy to imagine the effect that 210 bhp had on a car weighing, in this guise, only 975 kilograms (2,149 lb) – acceleration in 5.8 seconds from zero to 100 km/h (62.2 mph) and a top speed of 240 km/h (149 mph) were otherwise only to be had from outrageously expensive exotic cars.

78

At a time when driving a car was temporarily prohibited on Sundays and a speed limit of 100 km/h (62 mph), was in force, the desire for fast sports cars was rather subdued – but the Zuffenhausen manufacturer did not lose heart. The next step forward was the G-series 911, considerably modified for its 1974 launch. It could be identified visually by the flexible gaiters on the bumpers.

Beginning this year, all models had an engine of 2.7 liters' capacity and Bosch K-Jetronic fuel injection; there were new designations and new performance data: the basic model was the **911** with 150 bhp at 5,700 rpm and a top speed of 210 km/h (130 mph), then came the 911 S with 175 bhp at 5,800 rpm and 225 km/h (139 mph). The top model was now called the **911 Carrera**; it developed 210 bhp at 6,300 rpm and reached a top speed of 240 km/h (149 mph).

Since the Carrera RS was such an evident success, the Racing Department offered an even more powerful version at a price of 64,980 German Marks: the

Carrera RS 3.0 had a displacement of 2.994 cc and a power output of 230 bhp.

This was the first Porsche with a big rear wing and extremely wide fenders, which permitted the use of racing tires (eight inches wide at the front, nine at the back). The performance was best defined by the phenomenal time of 5.7 seconds from zero to 100 km/h (62.2 mph); the top speed of 238 km/h (148 mph) was just below that of the RS 2.7, since the flared fenders made the car considerably less aerodynamic. Production figures for the RS 3.0 were low, since the rules only required that 100 of the cars be built in order to obtain Group 4 homologation. In the end, there were 111 of them: 54 road cars, 42 RSR competition versions and 15 IROC cars that the American Roger Penske ordered for his "International Race of Champions."

In 1975, those who liked the wide tires and flared fenders on the RS 3.0 were offered the **911 Turbo** for the first time. Over the years, Porsche had been able to gather a lot of experience with tur-

bochargers in motor sport, and was therefore more than happy to make this principle available to power-hungry customers.

The first version of the Turbo, with a swept volume of 2.994 cc, developed 260 bhp at 5,500 rpm. The company now knew that its customers were willing to write checks for higher figures – so the Turbo was listed at 65,000 German Marks. For this money the customer could accelerate in 5.2 seconds from zero to 100 km/h (62.2 mph) and exult in a top speed of 260 km/h (162 mph).

In 1976, there were only three models in the line: the tried-and-true 911 with the 2.7-liter engine rated at 160 bhp, a new Carrera 3.0, now with a displacement of 2,994 cc and developing 200 bhp at 6,000 rpm, and the unchanged Turbo. Simultanously with these model changes Porsche became the first company in the world to guard actively against rust by using sheet metal galvanized on both sides for certain of the body panels.

79 ■ 1

Precisely 1,036 of the 210-horsepower Carrera model were built in 1974. The big rear spoiler was an option at extra charge

79 ■ 2

Reared on the race track: the 260 bhp Turbo

79 ■ 3

From 1977 on, the Turbo had 300 bhp and a top speed of 260 km/h (162 mph)

79 ■ 1

79 ■ 2

79 ■ 3

80 ■ 1

80 ■ 2

80 ■ 3

The next streamlining of the model line was planned for the Fall of 1977. Since with the 911, 924, and 928 the company now had three model lines, there were now only two 911 models: the 911 SC as a Coupé and Targa, and the Turbo Coupé.

SC, by the way, stood for the combination of the S model with the Carrera's power unit.

Knowing well that there were always people with a desire for ultimate high performance, Porsche ensured a further power boost for its Turbo model by increasing displacement to 3,299 cc and installing a charge-air intercooler: The fortunate owners of the **Turbo 3.3**, which could reach 260 km/h (162 mph), had 300 brake horsepower, available at 5,500 rpm, at their command.

In 1983 the 911 model range, in the meantime celebrating its twentieth birthday, acquired the **911 SC Cabriolet** as a long-awaited bonus. The first hint of this open-top car had been seen at the German Motor Show in 1981, when Porsche displayed a design study with

four-wheel drive and a turbocharged engine. So encouraging was the response that development finally started on adding the much-desired convertible model to the program.

Whereas the soft top still had to be opened and closed by hand on the first 911 Cabriolets, delivered in 1983, Porsche was working intensively on getting an electrically powered soft top ready for series production. This was a wish expressed by Ferry Porsche in particular.

The new Cabriolet proved extremely popular right from the start, and in subsequent years between 2,300 and 7,000 were sold annually, without any noticeable adverse effects on sales of the Targa, which remained in production.

In the two model years that followed, Porsche concentrated on minor improvements to its existing models. The 911 Carrera's engine size went up to 3,164 cc in 1984, with a parallel increase in power to 231 bhp. A year after this, the first 911 model appeared

with exhaust emission control by closed-loop, three-way catalytic converter, though involved reducing the amount of power at the customer's disposal to 207 bhp.

Customers had frequently expressed a desire to buy the basic models with the same flared fenders and wider tires as on the Turbo, and starting in the 1985 model year their wish was was granted. In the same way, the quest for more power was as vigorous as ever, and after another year had elapsed the option of purchasing the 3.3-liter Turbo as a Targa or Cabriolet became available. By 1989, 299 Turbo Targas and no fewer than 1,642 Turbo Cabriolets had been made and sold.

Then came the year 1986, and with it the **959**. Planned as a limited series of only 200 cars (though a further 84 were eventually built), this remarkable 911 derivative boasted every feature that the engineers and technicians were able to develop for and install within the limited confines of a somewhat modified 911 bodyshell. The 959's en-

80 ■ 1

*After an 18-year wait:
the 911 SC Cabriolet*

80 ■ 2

*Most powerful member of the tribe:
the 959 had a 450 bhp engine*

80 ■ 3

*As open as they come:
the Carrera Speedster of 1987*

gine had a displacement of 2,850 cc, but with the aid of twin turbochargers no fewer than 450 horsepower were coaxed out of it at 6,500 rpm. It was an artwork, but a most ingenious and practical one, as it proved in events as disparate as the Paris-Dakar Rally and the Le Mans 24-hour race. Wealthy customers fought to buy one: for 420,000 German Marks the 959 not only offered them permanent four-wheel drive but the awe-inspiring top speed of 315

production line, intended primarily for club-level racing activities. Priced at 82.275 German Marks, it was a much-lightened 911 (without noise insulating material, body cavity treatment or undersealing) with an engine permitted to run up to the higher speed of 6,840 rpm. With catalytic converter, it produced 217 bhp; without, 231 bhp. Of this spartan vehicle, 340 were sold in the years which followed, including a solitary Targa version.

rating from 0 to 100 km/h (62.2 mph) in only 5.7 seconds, the Carrera 4 was the fastest four-wheel-drive coupe on the market.

In the months which followed, other versions of the 964 series appeared: for 1990, it was also available as the Carrera 2, with conventional rear-wheel drive only. This not only resulted in a more agile car but also one that was about 100 kliograms (220 lb) lighter. A further notable development was the

81 • 1

81 • 2

81 • 3

km/h (195 mph) – from a car with all the day-to-day tractability of a typical Porsche. The 959 remains the incarnation of the leading-edge technology of its day, based admittedly on a 25-year-old concept but with no expense spared and no technical holds barred.

1987 saw the announcement of the Speedster, which with its spartan specification recalled the models Porsche had produced in the 1950s. Only 2,100 were made, including about 60 with a narrow body).

This was also the year in which the first 911 Carrera Club Sport Coupé left the

In the 1989 model year, major changes occurred. Porsche began to operate its new body plant, where the *Carrera 4*, the first car from the 964 series to appear, was also built.

Its body was distinctly different in appearance, and it was the first Porsche to be equipped with an extending rear spoiler, which swung up only at speeds in excess of 80 km/h (50 mph). The new-shape body was propelled by a further evolutionary stage in flat-six engine design, now with a swept volume of 3.6 liters and an output of 250 bhp. Good for a top speed of 260 km/h (161 mph) and capable of accele-

Tiptronic four-speed automatic transmission, which could also be shifted sequentially by hand.

With clear evidence at its disposal that customers desired and enjoyed cars of extreme sporting character, Porsche launched the next *Carrera RS* generation in the Fall of 1990. Extremely light in weight once again, at 1,240 kilograms (2,733 lb), and with its power output boosted to 260 bhp, no fewer than 2,279 of this model were sold. Launching the 964 series had led to production of the Turbo being halted in July 1989, and in fact it was not until

81 • 1

Now with four-wheel drive too:
the 1988 Carrera 4

81 • 2

Always the fastest:
in 1991 the Turbo developed
320 bhp

81 • 3

Emphatically light and sporting:
the 260 bhp Carrera RS

the Spring of 1991 that the next **911 Turbo** generation, based on the 964, actually appeared. Although equipped of necessity with a closed-loop, three-way catalytic converter, the 3.3-liter engine now developed 320 bhp at 5,750 rpm. The car's qualities were undusputed, in particular its new standards of environmental acceptability, but there was none the less some discussion as to whether its performance was adequate. After all, the regular

1993 was "Turbo year", so to speak – the new 3.6-liter version developed an impressive 360 brake horsepower at 5,500 rpm. Those who felt even this to be insufficient were able to bid for a limited-edition **Turbo S**, of which only 80 were built; it had a power output of 381 bhp, could reach 295 km/h (183 mph) and cost 295,000 German Marks.

The second-generation, 964-based

The 993 was effectively a new car, both visually and technically. After a great deal of detail design work, its engine now developed 272 horsepower. The six-speed gearbox was also new, and within a short time a four-wheel-drive version with the familiar Carrera 4 model name was also offered.

A number of new models followed in 1995: the latest 911 Targa was premiered, satisfying open-car enthusiasts'

82∎1

82∎2

82∎3

Coupe was itself capable of reaching 260 km/h (161 mph) – and at 178,500 German Marks, the Turbo was far from cheap.

The technical team therefore tackled the task of boosting the Turbo's power output with some urgency. The result was the Turbo 3.6, but before this appeared, in 1992, the company announced the next Carrera RS, with a more powerful naturally aspirated engine, also of 3.6 liters'capacity. The Cup version was offered at 148,000 German Marks and developed a healthy 275 bhp. 112 were built.

Speedster also appeared in this model year. At first, it was only available with the narrow, Cabriolet-style body and cost 131,500 German Marks, saving 8,457 Marks compared with the more luxuriously equipped Cabriolet. The customers took this badly: they wanted their **Carrera Speedsters** to have the wider Turbo body style as well. Porsche acceded to this wish, and by the end of 1993 had built 930 of this version of the Speedster.

Late in 1993 the next **Carrera** generation, designated internally as the 993, began to reach Porsche dealers.

wishes with a large glass roof panel which retracted behind the rear window when opened.

The biggest sensation, however, was the new **911 Turbo**, based on the Carrera 4 with its permanent four-wheel drive, and with a 408 bhp engine deriving its thrust from twin turbochargers.

The new Turbo was not only fascinating in terms of its almost unbelievable power and its top speed of well over 300 km/h (186 mph), but also because these achievements were allied to exceptionally good roadholding.

This led in the first magazine reports to

82∎1
Only 80 of these 381 bhp Turbo S models were built

82∎2
In 1993 the second Speedster generation appeared

82∎3
Also in 1993, the 993 was launched in Coupé and Carrera versions

initial comparisons with the legendary Porsche 959 being made.

Porsche continued to serve active motor sport enthusiasts well. An improved Carrera RS with 300 bhp, 3.8-liter engine was produced. Then came the GT 2, a competition version of the 911 with turbocharged 430 bhp engine. This was a most remarkable hybrid – 172 customers ordered one as a road car, another 65 for competition use.

a close. The air-cooled engine had increasing difficulty in coping with today's tough exhaust and noise emission regulations, to say nothing of those still to come. A change to liquid cooling was inevitable. In Porsche's typical way, the necessary know-how was obtained from racing engines, and the first series product to feature the new engine was the Boxster, introduced successfully in the Summer of 1996 with a 204 bhp, 2.5-liter engine.

for the fact that progress not only means more vigorous performance from a smaller-size engine, but also a ten percent improvement in fuel consumption compared with the previous car.

New but eternally young: it's good to know that the latest 911 model will be joined before long by various other versions.

The Cabriolet is already with us: it had its world premiere in March 1998 at the

83▪1

83▪2

83▪3

Probably the most potent 911 version of all, however, was the GT 1, which Porsche decided to build in 1996 in order to contest the World GT Championship. Since at least one road car had to be built for homologation purposes, the GT 1 was licensed for the road and a few of these 544 bhp cars were let loose on the public. Demand has been tempered by the fact that although the car was capable of 310 km/h (192 mph), it cost well over a million German Marks.

Observers of the 911 scene were only too well aware that the era of the "classic" model was rapidly drawing to

In September 1997 the long-awaited new Porsche *911* was to be seen at the German Motor Show in Frankfurt. It is larger, more spacious and more comfortable than before, but is still propelled by a flat-six "boxer" engine at the rear, though this is now water-cooled and produces 300 bhp from a swept volume of 3,387 cc. Viewed critically at first, the new car's performance data are surely one of the best arguments in its favor: zero to 100 km/h (62.2 mph) in 5.2 seconds, zero to 200 km/h (124 mph) in 19.6 seconds and a top speed of 280 km/h (174 mph). The new Carrera is a visually convincing argument

Geneva Motor Show; the new Carrera 4 is expected to appear in the Fall of 1998, and well before the millennium draws to a close, there will also be a new Turbo.

The air-cooled flat-six engine, of which about 400,000 had been built by the end of 1997, will not be dispatched to its well-earned retirement until the next century starts. By then, it will have been making its contribution to our driving pleasure for almost forty years. Four decades in which a truly exceptional engine and a superb concept reached an impressive level of maturity and acquired the status of an icon.

Super Grade Please!

by Clauspeter Becker

THE WORLD OF ENGINE POWER acquired a whole new dimension in 1985. Those who were accustomed to feeling the power of an internal combustion engine develop in a strong, smooth flow – regardless of its rated power – were (and are) confronted with a new and uncommonly exciting form of power from the Porsche 959. In this car, instead of the familiar thrust, you get the impression that the tail is equipped with nearly inexhaustible reserves of multi-stage rockets, ignited by mere pressure on the accelerator pedal. And it happens again in every gear.

Acceleration in this car is like taking a ride over three power curves. We owe this unique experience to technology that, like a short-lived comet, quickly burned out on its path into the future. The Porsche 959 is the first and only production car with multi-stage forced aspiration, which builds up boost pressure and torque in three stages. Select a gear at low engine speeds, and you first experience a phase of natural induction (but by no means of passive reflection). At about 2,500 revolutions, turbocharger number one gives you the first violent kick in the back. After that, there is little time to recover: in the 4,500 revs zone, turbocharger number two reports for duty with a big push and a most awe-inspiring sound from the back of the car.

Even in those early days of heavy metal music, an even louder level for the turbocharged trumpet concert was possible. The muffler was occasionally (and secretly) taken off the second turbocharger, which then produced an inferno of noise and with it a further healthy increase in power.

Today, 18 years later, there are not just Porsches but also other cars that accelerate better than a 959. But there has never been such a dramatic presentation of performance, nor such a modulated engine sound that creates such excitement. These wild sides of the super-Porsche of the past were, at the time, by-products, maybe even undesirable ones. It was not until it started its second career that the 959 became a perfect, cultured monument to everything that is technically feasible.

These never fully tamed machinations came from its sporty youth, from a time when people at the factory were still giving the 959 the "Group B" title. It was intended as the ultimate competition car, strong and fierce enough to swallow alive the muscle-bound, four-wheel-drive beasts from Audi, Lancia or Ford. But then the F.I.A., that well-meaning sport authority, showed some insight, put a stop to this power play with 600 (or maybe even more) horsepower and guided the rules back to a level closer to the average production car.

The Porsche 959 Supercar, already very well advanced technically, needed a new job. Professor Helmut Bott, Wolfhelm Gorissen and Manfred Bantle decided to give the car a new role as technical flagship; the Porsche 959 was to represent the top technology of the 1980s. In those days, many a task was solved with tremendous effort – a fact which soon taught the company that many things can be achieved equally well with greater simplicity. The engine is a good example of mechanical engineering based on the motto: we only use the best of everything.

It was of course based on the flat-six "boxer" design. Nevertheless, this engine's original configuration for racing was the reason for its relatively small displacement (due to the relation between displacement and weight in the regulations). It took a lot of new technological tricks to charm the desired 450 bhp (331 kW) out of it.

959

84 ▪ 1

84 ▪ 1
An exclusive instrument arrangement in the Porsche 959: a tachometer up to 8,500/min, a charge-pressure gauge to 2.0 bar, and a speedometer up to 340 km/h

85 ▪ 1
Despite its very sporty character, the 959 still had the natural charm and serious note that marks all 911s and sets them apart from other sports cars

85 ■ 1

86■4

86■3

86■1

86■5

86■2

86■6

Studio Farr

87■4

87■

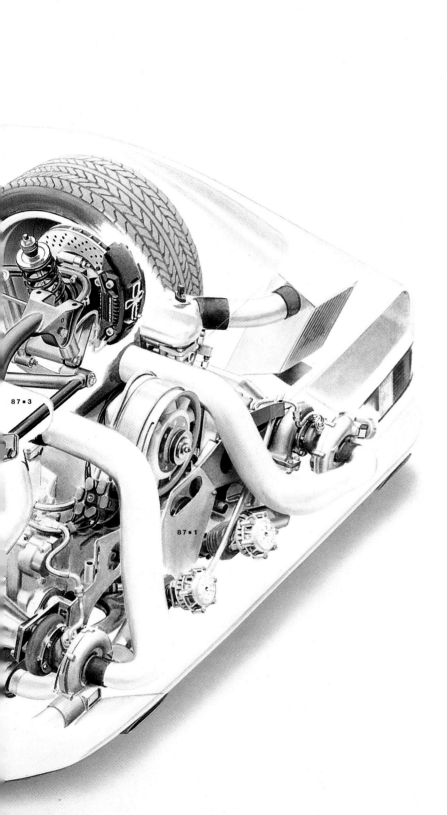

THE ICON
The high-tech giant: 959

87 ■ 1

Six-cylinder, 2,850 cc "boxer" engine with two turbochargers for multi-stage forced aspiration, output 450 bhp (331 kW) at 6,500 rpm, torque: 500 Newton-meters (369 lb.ft.) at 5,500 rpm

87 ■ 2

Water-cooled cylinder heads, each with chain-driven double overhead camshafts, four valves per cylinder, air-cooled cylinders, two charge-air intercoolers

87 ■ 3

Rear suspension with double wishbones, two Bilstein gas-filled shock absorberson each side, one with spring, one with hydropneumatic self-leveling

86 ■ 1

Front suspension with double wishbones,two Bilstein gas-filled shock absorbers on each side, both with springs, one with hydropneumatic self-leveling; 235/40 ZR 17 tires

86 ■ 2

Six-speed manual transmission with additional drive to front axle

86 ■ 3

Housing for front differential and hydraulically actuated multi-disc clutch for power distribution to the front axle

86 ■ 4

Radiators for cooling circuits for the two cylinder heads

86 ■ 5

Power-assisted rack-and-pinion steering

87 ■ 4

Light-alloy weels with hollow cast spokes and inductive tire-pressure monitoring. Rims: 9 J 17,tires: 255/35 ZR 17. The vented covers were for the racing version

86 ■ 6

Front wheels with 8 J 17 rims and 235/40 ZR 17 Bridgestone RE 71 road tires

The 1985-period cylinder heads are still state-of-the-art today: water-cooling, double overhead camshafts, four valves per cylinder. The air-cooled cylinders were more for the sake of tradition than technology. Multi-stage turbocharging was an attempt to overcome turbo lag, which at the time was still severe enough to notice. If you compare the figures from back then with those of today, the 959 could develop 450 bhp (331 kW) at 6,500 rpm, and 500 Newton-meters (369 lb.ft.) of torque at 5,500 rpm. A 1998 Porsche Turbo with a swept volume of 3.6 liters, but with classic, air-cooled, two-valve heads and two turbochargers (without multi-stage turbocharging) turns out 430 bhp (316 kW) at 5,750 rpm and devlops a torque of 550 Newton-meters (406 lb.ft.) at 4,500 rpm.

The four-wheel drive is another technological wonder. Power distribution to the front axle is controlled by a highly-intelligent system. The ABS sensors on each of the four wheels keep their eyes open for slip. An electronic computer analyzes the data. Based on the commands from this unit, a hydraulic system regulates the power flow to the front wheels via a multi-disc clutch. There is also a differential lock on the rear axle that can be varied electrohydraulically in its locking action. Besides all the advice from the electronics, the 959 offers the driver a chance to select various traction programs. No other Porsche driveline has ever had this level of complexity: current four-wheel drive models are content with a viscous coupling that controls power distribution most effectively without any intervention by the electronics or the driver.

In 1985, the electronics ruled in the chassis and suspension areas too. On the 959, computer-controlled ride-height control and shock absorber adjustment are in danger of stealing the limelight from what is really important. The sensational driving characteristics are due primarily to the new suspension, with double wishbones on the front and rear axle. It becomes clear what the new 911 proved in 1993 by more simple means: the seemingly unlimited potential offered by a rear-engined car in conjunction with good suspension design.

In 1985, the Porsche 959's body gave us a look at a future which was still taking shape. We could already see the trend towards flatter front fenders, the air ducting for the radiators, and the spoiler integrated into the tail. Until that time no 911 had ever reached the width of the 959: 1,840 mm. Nor were subsequent cars able to match its aerodynamic qualities: the body of the 959 is free of any lifting forces, a fact which lends it a level of safety and calmness at 300 km/h (186 mph) that Walter Röhrl still considers to be unsurpassed.

Although the 959's sports career was regulated out of existence, the Super-Porsche did harvest some of the glory it deserved: it won, for instance, the 1986 Paris-Dakar Desert Rally. Businesswise, the balance sheet for this technological flagship ended with 283 cars sold, most of which now lead quiet, wear-free lives as collector's items. For Porsche itself, the most expensive version of the 911 brought no profit: production costs for a 959 were approximately twice as high as its selling price of 450,000 German Marks.

Nevertheless, this expensive experiment was surely worth the effort: during its development career, the 959 proved to be the father of all modern 911's in the 1990s. It not only had everything needed for the future, it also revealed what was superfluous. Like many supercars of its day, the Porsche 959 ended up not becoming an object of speculation after all. It still remains something of a bargain. In nearly new condition, it can be purchased at prices beginning at about 365,000 German marks, and offers more high technology for the money than can otherwise be had for this price.

89▪1
A close look at the Porsche 959 in the mid 1980s was a glimpse of the future. It possessed the fender outline also found on later models, and the voluminous air slots with radiators breathing through them for the first time

90■1

90 ■ 1

In the 959, the rotary fan that is typical of Porsche "boxer" engines now feeds cool air only to the six cylinders. The cylinder heads are water cooled

91 ■ 1

Anti-skid seats for the 959's driver and passenger: instead of leather, woolen cloth upholstery was available at no extra charge for those who preferred it

91 ■ 2

A 959 is a rare sight on public roads in broad daylight. Museums and the air-conditioned garages of rich collectors are now its natural habitat

91 ■ 3

In 1985, the 959's aerodynamics represented an ideal for fast drivers. Lift was zero at both axles. The result: perfect road grip

91 ■ 1

91 ■ 2

91 ■ 3

By Michael Köckritz

Pure Emotions

The kind of people wo live for and with Porsche

Herbert Linge

1954. Together with Helmut Polensky, "Mister Weissach" took part in the (in)famous long-distance marathon Liège-Rom-Liège – and after four days and nights, ended it at precisely the spot he never thought he would reach in his wildest dreams (after all, this was the very first of all for this Porsche 356 aluminium-bodied coupé and the four-camshaft engine from the Spider). On the winner's podium! Totally exhausted but overjoyed, with the trophy and a cigar held tightly in his hand.

Maybe this success was also due to the fact that the two men had been able to test the new racer extensively beforehand – as they drove to the starting point or, as Linge says with greater accuracy: "testing in transit."

But that's how things were for someone who was not able to earn a living from racing alone. This privilege was reserved for just a few world-class drivers. "Fees were hardly ever paid at that time, and the prize money was usually only enough to cover travel expenses." So Linge kept his job at Porsche.

His impressive 15-year motor sport career stands in contrast to his 45-year life as a model Porsche-person. Herbert Linge spent all his working years at Porsche. Beginning in 1943 (the strict Professor himself accepted him as an apprentice when he was a 15 year old with excellent school grades and a strong interest in cars and technology), right up to his official farewell in 1987 as manager of the experimental workshops at the Weissach development center.

In this case "official" meant that he was still able to serve another three years as a valued advisor to "his company." With a biography like that, you automatically become a permanent part of the Porsche myth. Not to mention the fact that Herbert Linge knows every tiny detail of the story, how it came about – and what to think of it. First there are the cars. The 356, 911 – again and again the 911 – the racing cars, the big successes: Linge experienced the Mille Miglia, the German racing championships, the world manufacturers' championships, Le Mans, and all the other victories in close-up.

Porsche, says Linge today, is above all the unique miracle of how a small family business – the "workshop" in Zuffenhausen, where the product alone was always the focus of every thought and action – could become one of the great makes in automotive history. "I expect it was precisely this no-compromise zeal that made everything else possible," Herbert Linge adds pensively as he fishes a cigar out of the box.

His in-depth experience as a Porsche test driver and enthusiasm for fast driving predestined Herbert Linge early on as a specialist for long distances. Even better – his sound training as a mechanic gave him additional qualifications. After all, he had been accepted as an apprentice by Ferdinand Porsche himself

successful companies of all when it comes to satisfying secondary needs with luxury items, time is the very essence of personal luxury.

Leisure time. Time that opens up freedom for the soul, time to find yourself, time for family or friends. Or time for the car. His first choice of course would be one of the Porsches he loves so passionately. In this way, luxury loses all its culpable and superfluous character. The reward becomes a necessary, primary need; the object of luxury is used consciously at the right moment as a point of crystalization for the soul. Even Carla Bruni suddenly seems a trace more captivating.

Karl-Friedrich Scheufele

And finally, at the very end of the conversation, one last question – in order to get a balanced, clear picture.
Mr. Scheufele, how do you define personal luxury?

The well-groomed forty year old, standing under two black & white publicity photographs of Carla Bruni (wearing sparkling jewlery and looking captivating as always) only has to think for a moment. Then a boyish smile reveals that he has come up with the answer that fits him perfectly: Time!
For Karl-Friedrich Scheufele, Vice-President of Chopard, one of the most

He received his first car from his parents. As a present. A Beetle Cabriolet. Not new, but painted in a striking yellow. Almost a Porsche.
The first real one followed a short time later. The 356 Cabriolet was an ivory-colored used car. Well used, to be honest – as its catastrophic condition signaled from a good distance. But financed with the first money he had earned himself. And above all: A PORSCHE! That was all that mattered back then.
Looking back, one can admit that, in light of peripheral mechanical conditions on the periphery, it must have been an extremely dangerous relationship. His parents, in any event,

were extremely concerned. And rightfully so, as it became clear once the car – after some years of service (or fun, to be more accurate) – was sold to another enthusiast. He had no problem driving his new racer home. It wasn't until he arrived at the garage that the rear axle broke. Which, of course, the new owner reported right away. But not to let off steam in deep annoyance, just for information. That's passion – and typical of the true Porsche enthusiast, as Scheufele explains.

Just as typical: the logical goal of all Porsche passion that is lived out consistently: driving a 911. Scheufele achieved that at the early age of 28. "A super car. No compromises. With character. But you had to do your best to avoid driving errors."
Karl-Friedrich Scheufele learned that lesson as he (trembling but unharmed) struggled on foot out of the field into which he had drifted – in a brief burst of over-confidence – with his 911S. More important than his own condition: the car was hardly damaged at all … .

Today, four or five 911s later, there is a 993 Cabriolet in the garage. It stands next to the 356 Speedster from the early A-series in top condition, which will never be sold again, if his wife has her way. But the promise was already made long ago.

When we encounter watches or cars in the zone beyond all the demands of everyday life, time and timeless elegance quickly become overlapping circles of existence. The Vice President of Chopard, Karl-Friedrich Scheufele, lives in masterful coexistence with these elementary axioms of our souls

Questionnaire for a Porsche person – loosely based on Marcel Proust and the honorable example of "FAZ-Magazin."

Hervé Fontaine

What is absolute happiness for you, as a car person?
To sit in my Formula 1 car and drive it up to MY limit.

What faults are you most likely to forgive a car?
None!

What is your favorite car in everyday life?
My Mercedes 500E.

…and in your free time?
Any pure-bred race car on a track.

Your favorite figure in automotive history?
Ferdinand Porsche.

What characteristics to you appreciate the most in a car?
Reliability.

What characteristics do you most admire in a driver?
Common sense, concentration, and the ability to anticipate.

What characteristics do you most admire in a woman driver?
All the characteristics that I also admire in men – plus a certain attractiveness.

Your main characteristic as a driver?
Patience.

Your biggest mistake as a driver?
A spin-out at 150 kilometers an hour in a friend's Ferrari F50. It ruined four tires and four rims.

Your favorite activity connected with cars?
Porsche CK5, Group C, and my two Formula 1 racing cars.

Who or what would you like to have been in the car world?
Gerhard Mitter in a hill climb.

What car invention do you most appreciate?
All the extras that enhance passive safety.

What car invention do you dislike the most?
The rigid rear axle.

What's the best road movie?
"Le Mans" with Steve McQueen.

What race would you like to win some day?
LeMans.

… and in which event would you never take part?
I'd never enter a rally. I'd be too afraid.

Your favorite color for your everyday car?
Silver metallic.

…and for your dream car?
Black.

Your favorite car designer?
Pininfarina.

Your favorite hero in automotive history?
Ayrton Senna.

Your role model as a car person?
Ferdinand Porsche.

Your driving motto?
In slowly, out quickly!

A Job Opening in Africa

by Herbert Völker

911 SC

THIS IS A STORY about not winning, and it has about seventeen beginnings and a short ending.

The Taita hills are a good example of an early beginning: four million years before the invention of the wheel. Ever since then, they have been jutting abruptly out of the Savanna plain; it's the type of surprise we call the Kilimanjaro effect – which can be verified by its prototype about 200 kilometers (124 miles) to the northwest. For the Safari Rally, the Taitas have always been the bad hills. They can be seen from a long way off, and convey a far from pleasant feeling. They tower up as if the devil had built himself a stronghold. They penetrate the clouds and collect five times as much rain as the plains right next to them. That gives them their own climate, their own plants, their own animals, and their own tribe of humans with a language also called Taita.

The Taita Hills swallow up rally cars on their south loop, and after, say, three hours, spit them back out again on the other side. If the cars are lucky.

Another beginning for our story:

"The merciless conditions were due to the intensity of the falling snow, which made it difficult to make progress (particularly for less-powerful cars), limited visibility to just a few yards, made the fatigued eyes of the drivers (who had been on the road for more than two days) even redder, and drove them to the point of complete exhaustion." This is contemporary prose describing the Monte Carlo Rally in 1965, when it snowed more fearsomely then it ever would again for (at least) the next 33 years. As fate would have it, this happened to be the occasion for which Eugen Böhringer had been given a Porsche 904, a race car modified more or less for use on public roads, at least on paper.

Of the 237 cars that started the race, only 24 made it to the finishing line at all. That's how devastating the situation was. But the beautiful plastic-bodied beast was among the finishers. What's more: it was only beaten by the incomparable Timo Mäkinen, and he drove a Mini Cooper. (Hey friends, can you imagine how they looked: the Mini Cooper with the hawk-like Timo Mäkinen, and the Porsche, with the heavily-built Eugen. All around it's snowing so hard that you don't even know whether your driving up or down a hill. The cars cannon off snowbanks, the drivers let loose a string of curses to match the weather – one of them in Finnish, the other in Swabian dialect. Then you have to imagine that behind them a Saab 96 is thundering through the desert snowscape. Inside sits the young Pat Moss (Stirling's sister), and she is pushing the accelerator down like a wounded lioness. Her navigator is the blond Liz Nyström, who bowled our reporter over completely and utterly back then: "so very young, pretty as a picture, and unbelievably delicate." So here we are: Timo in the Cooper, Eugen in the 904, Pat and the unbelievably delicate Liz in the Saab, all of them flying blind through the night. Isn't that enough to bring a tear to your eye?).

Huschke von Hanstein, who, as always, made a good impression back then as Porsche race manager, was allegedly not at all amused about finishing second – which provides with us another possible beginning for our story: a lack of humility.

Key men in the Porsche world considered rallies to be the weaker brother of car racing, and anyone who could win races would easily manage a rally or two as well. Even Ferdinand Piëch, (who would now be about to enter the scene with the Porsche 906, if this were our subject here), did not abandon this elevated standpoint until 15 years later, after he had been at Audi for quite some time.

Another beginning: In that snow-blown year of 1965, the first works 911 was also on the circuit. It was green on the outside and equipped on the inside with master mechanic Herbert Linge and engineer Peter Falk, both from the Porsche testing department. Their job was really just to find out how the thing drove, and whether it had any bugs. Linge's comment was that the tail sometimes prefers to lead the way, and then you have to catch it. Apart from that, he took fifth place in the class. That was indeed quite nice, but in Huschke's eyes, not a sufficient argument against the rule that motor sport takes place primarily on race tracks.

The story also has a Swedish beginning: On November 12, 1943, in the village of Rolshagen, a delightful little boy was born, and named Björn. At the age of seven, he was allowed to drive around on the farm in a Saab, which gave him a feeling for machinery of the mobile kind. It just so happened that by the time he got a license, Swedish rally sport was just beginning to reach its peak: Erik Carlsson was a mobile monument, the works teams from Saab and Volvo laid down what was state of the art, and young Mr. Källström whisked so quietly through the forests in a Beetle, that people began to speak of a whispering revolution. This was when the driving-in-a-higher-gear principle was invented, which states that it is better to exploit momentum than to brake and shift – which seemed logical enough to the world's young people. It was in this healthy atmosphere that Björn Waldegård learned the tools of his trade.

THE ICON
Rallying: the 911 SC "Safari"

100■1

100■1

While it is true that in 1978 there was neither a Rally Department nor a Porsche works driver, the energy of all concerned, and the experience gained from earlier events made it possible to create a works car, from the concept to the last detail, as though there had never been even the shortest of interruptions in the company's rally involvement

101■1

"It looked very courageous, high on its wheels and in the Martini colors. It was probably the most endearing piece of machinery ever to have been pushed out into the great flood"

102■1

102■2

102■3

THE ICON
Rallying: The 911 SC "Safari"

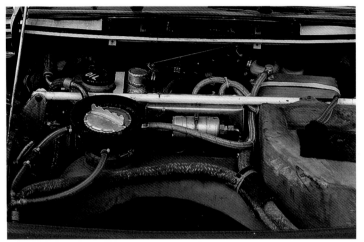

104 ■ 2

It was probably the importers and private entrants who made themselves so obnoxious that they caused a reversal to take place in the motor sport policy of half-hearted casualness. From 1968 on, Porsche mounted a works rally team. At first it was still under the reins of Huschke von Hanstein, but Rico Steinemann took over in 1969.

These crack troops, as slim and powerful as their cars, ruthlessly swept away all the former standards in rally sport. It was the most favorable moment imaginable for this feat of strength: Thanks to the works teams from Ford, Lancia, Alpine, Porsche, and Saab, nearly all of Europe was involved in the action, and a cult-era of emotional motor sport – also with very special aesthetic appeal – was able to develop. What we would define as the direct injection of technical intellect was now in such a highly evolved condition at Porsche that it had no difficulty adapting to the new element:

104 ■ 1/2

Structural rigidity and crew protection are everything in the Safari. Nevertheless, relatively few visible elements had to be added. The bulwark largely took the form of internal structural measures

The car has to be fast, the car has to make it to the end, whether on the Col du Turini or on the race track.

By the time that this sweet, feverish dream came to an end, Porsche had won the Monte Carlo Rally three times running, and indeed most other events held to be important, including the World Manufacturers' Championship. Of the half a dozen drivers who maintained this furious pace, one emerged who like things hotter than all the others: Björn Waldegård. He was the quintessence of that unifying spiritual force, a personal union of traction and drive without any unneccessary components.

To keep the trees from growing into the heavens, the Type 914/6 was created and even sent to the 1971 Monte Carlo Rally. Of course this did not work, and the break could hardly have been more dramatic: instead of using the heaven-storming nature of the 911 and making it (as the Carrera then) by far the most successful rally car in history, Porsche's involvement ran aground in money-saving programs and lost its direction. At least they were still able to say officially: "We have already won everything, what more should we do?"

The Safari, friends, just the Safari.

Here is how the legend goes: This is the toughest test for cars, and only the humble can win. To this, the people in Zuffenhausen basically said "Sure," then put up the proudest cars ever to cross the equator. That was in 1971, and everything was just right. Waldegård was already leading by a half an hour – but somehow the humility thing did not seem to have penetrated all the way to the inner core. In the thick dust of the car about to be passed, there was a crash, and not one between a Porsche and another make, but between Porsche and Porsche. Deep pain. A Datsun 240 Z won. Even deeper pain. In those years, the crumple zone of Porsche's contentment ended very abruptly when faced with Japanese hardware.

In the months and years to come, the Rally Department dematerialized itself, so to speak. Not a single driver was kept under contract. The replacement for the Rally Department concept was called Jürgen Barth. Thanks to his connections with private entrants, he was at least able to constantly report on how anxious the best or the best-sponsored drivers were to take part in rallies at the wheel of a Porsche. Furthermore, from time to time he was able to issue a reminder about something that had been left undone.

"There's also the question of the Safari."

In 1973, green light was given again, but there was no warm-up, and once again, no humility (at least not among Barth and the drivers). There was not a single serious test, just some small Safari-relevant modifications, and the result was a disaster in the transmission and shock absorber department. When a Japanese car won again, a mood arose in Zuffenhausen that we will call constructive doggedness: This couldn't be the answer.

So they returned the next year, but this time with top cars and a motivated team. Waldegård was about a light year ahead, and four fifths of the rally were over, then the rear axle link broke. Jürgen Barth was right on the scene and was able to repair it, but it just wasn't enough. The second place finish was received with great frustration in Stuttgart, exacerbated by the fact that they were not even able to spell the name of the Japanese make that won this time; to be honest, it was a nightmare.

That would have been the end of the matter had it not been for a nagging conscience. In the meantime, even a manufacturer of heavy luxury sedans from the Stuttgart area made a grab for Safari laurels. Were the Masters of the Universe to ignore people telling them that there was still a job opening in Africa?

Which brings us to the year 1978. As though with a deliberate mocking gesture, Jean-Pierre Nicolas won the Monte Carlo rally in a Carrera owned by the Almeras brothers.

106∎1   106∎2

From a standing start, so to speak – that's how superior the 911 was in normal rallies. How many victories it could have harvested over the the years! But none of this meant much when it came to the Safari.

While its true that Porsche no longer had a Rally Department, it did have two guys that were like an entire department in themselves: Jürgen Barth and Roland Kussmaul set up the strategy, handled the logistics, raised the funds, sang their song to the Board of Management, conducted tests, made service plans (for the equally motivated mechanics, who were all hewn from the same wood), and finally, jumped into an SC and slammed through six thousand kilometers at rally tempo. There was not a screw on the car they didn't know.

It was clear to all involved that the project would only make sense if they could get Björn Waldegård for the job. He had been without a home at Porsche for the past seven years, with the exception of guest appearances in the in-between Safaris, and had since lived through all difficulties of a legionnaire's life, with Citroën and BMW, Fiat and Toyota, Lancia and Ford. In a Stratos, he had put the great Munari's nose out of joint, and in an Escort, had won the Safari up front. And yet: Waldegård was Porsche.

And so Porsche made a call to Ford, and they released Björn and his colleague, the excellent Hans Thorszelius, for the 1978 Safari. As driver number two, they chose the young Vic Preston, who also made a contribution to the network with his local logistics. The Porsche SC had the three-liter

engine rated at 250 bhp, and looked very bold with its high stance and the Martini colors. It was probably the most appealing piece of machinery ever to have been forced out into the mighty flood waters.

For it was indeed a great flood. At the river crossings, the Mercedes engines gurgled and wept. Rear engines float better, as we may once have learned in our physics lessons. A vulture slammed into Björn's windshield, Barth and Kussmaul were ready with first aid, and Björn stormed off again.

Waldegård had a 46 minute lead over the rest of the field (insofar as it was not already drowned or demolished) as he turned from Mackinnon Road onto the path that led to the Taita Hills. These tower up, as we have read, as if the devil had built himself a stronghold, and even the fastest service teams can only drive around them and wait on the other side.

Björn, oh Björn: here he comes, dragging himself along on three wheels. Broken rear axle trailing arm. For the first time in the Safari it was made of aluminum; you always have to keep improving. They had coated the arm with fiberglass to protect it against minor injuries. While switching from one rocky lane to another, all at the most terrifying speed, it happened anyway: "Sensitivity to striking curbs," it said in the report sent back to the folks at home.

Barth and Kussmaul replaced the arm on the edge of the Taita Hills, and Björn shot off northward like the devil, stormed towards Suswa, entered the last night near Naivasha, went around the lake, conquered the Mau mountains, raced into the unpopulated north, entered settled land near Archers Post, went around Mount Kenya, and reported back to Nairobi. But it was too late.

We'll be back, the Porsche people said, but it wasn't true. Later they built a 911 that was able to drive much longer and much faster. They cured that car of succumbing to curb hits, and won the Paris – Dakar with it, and then again with the 959, so that in the end, all was proved that had to be proved – but that was a different story.

CHAPTER 5

Single-seaters

The story began in 1957, with the passenger's seat of the Spyder RS neatly covered over. Two years later the first Porsche Formula 2 racing car went to the starting grid in Monaco, only to crash heavily after two laps. Then came 1960, and a rich harvest: victory in the manufacturers' world championship.

The post-war period of brilliant improvisation was over – Formula 1, with its 1500 cc engines, called for high-tech, high outputs per liter and engine speeds up to and beyond 10,000 revolutions a minute. The new eight-cylinder engine performed well, but was so far removed from any production model that Porsche decided to decline the challenge. Then came 1983, and the second Formula 1 era, with Porsche as the designers of the TAG engine, the most successful German Formula 1 power source ever and an instant technical milestone in the age of turbocharging.

804
The engine survived the car for a further six seasons

TAG TURBO
Technical yardstick for a whole generation

CISITALIA
Well ahead of its time, though few were aware of it

FORMULA 2
Moss, Bonnier and Hill took the Type 718 to victory in the manufacturers' world championship

CIS 360

WITHOUT START, WITHOUT VICTORY
THE MOST ADVENTUROUS OF ALL GRAND PRIX CARS WAS FAR AHEAD
OF ITS TIME – IF ONLY WE HAD KNOWN

by David Staretz

"MY FATHER'S FAMOUS CIS models lie in chains, but the *racing wildcats*, as they were called, will soon roar again …My mother – who by the way was one of the most beautiful women in Turin – has sold her glorious town house at least to partially satisfy my father's creditors …I am just returning from negotiations with our many good friends …Cisitalia will reconquer its world fame, the car with the fastest times will not be defeated by its competitor Mammon and will again earn the victory laurels."

Somehow you can sense and feel the confused emptiness of these words – quotes from an interview that journalist Pitt Schultes conducted in the 1950s with Carletto, the son of industrial magnate and sportsman Piero Dusio.

The conversation appeared at the end of a long and promising story about Porsche's most unfortunate (but from today's perspective, most valuable) Grand Prix car, the Type 360.

Among its potential opponents in the post-war era (Mercedes, Ferrari, Maserati, and the Alfas!) it represented the peak of racing car development, though relaxed and completely in step with the company's trim style; a brilliant Porsche design through and through:

– with the horizontally opposed 12-cylinder mid-engine set deeply in the frame (competitors were still driving cars with the power units up front)

– with four-wheel drive, and the ability to disconnect the drive to the front wheels while in motion

– with a five-speed synchromesh transmission that had only two gate planes – like a motorcycle gear shift

– with four independently suspended wheels, based in the front on the parallel trailing-arm layout from Auto Union's racing cars (a Porsche design!). In the rear there was a double swing axle in accordance with the principle seen on the early Volkswagen

– with an aluminium body over a chrome-molybdenum steel frame and a weight of just 630 kg (1,389 lb).

Ideally it would have been possible to obtain a power to weight ratio of 1.4 kg (3.1 lb)/bhp – provided that the engine produced the 450 bhp at 10,500 revs that it was calculated as developing when in top form. Something to keep in mind:

At that time there was a 1.5-liter displacement limit, but mechanical supercharging was allowed (Porsche used Roots or Centrik superchargers at boost pressures of approximately 1.8 bar). The fuel question was dealt with liberally, which is why a racing fuel mixture with an octane level of 150 was assumed to be available.

The fact that the quoted power ratings (theoretical, practical, on the testing rig, or idealized) are so far apart is in the nature of the matter. 280 bhp, 363 bhp, 385 bhp, 450 bhp with an option for 500 – the figure was of little significance. The car was never really able to demonstrate its abilities.

Its long, unfullfilled story began when businessman Piero Dusio from Turin gained some respectable sports successes with his own Cisitalia marque.

108 ▪ 1

This front end was supposed to become one of the most famous in the history of the automobile – but a chain of circumstances made the car one of the greatest Porsche rarities in history

109

SINGLE-SEATERS
The Cisitalia adventure

*Melancholy pictures from
Normandy, somehow recalling a
stranded whale. During a test drive
in Buenos Aires, the tail fin flew off.
Something which was not difficult
to imagine.
In the meantime, the car (a museum
piece now) is in the best condition
of its life – just a few decades
too late*

The little CIS with a Fiat 1,100-cc engine, something of a post-war Formula Junior race car, was driven successfully by people like Nuvolari, Taruffi, Stuck, and above all, Bonetto.

Cisitalia's rise to the Grand Prix league seemed to be a natural development.

Cooperation with the Porsche design office came about-through the engineers' grapevine, members of which were the two Austrians Rudolf Hruschka (later to develop the Alfa-sud) and Carlo Abarth. Later they were joined by Eberan von Eberhorst, the man with Auto Union Grand Prix experience, (who later fell out with Carlo Abarth). Nuvolari and Millanta, an Italian automotive journalist, established important contacts, but only the top man, Ferdinand Porsche, was still unreachable in French custody.

On December 20, 1946 Dusio met with Porsche's people in Kitzbühel: Ferry (Ferdinand's son), his sister Louise Piëch, and chief designer Karl Rabe.

Besides more remote projects they agreed to work on the plans for a top-class GP racing car, and to supervize construction of the car in the Cisitalia works in Turin.

The engineering team consisting of Porsche, Schmid (transmission), Komenda (body), and Mickl (calculations) worked under Project Manager Karl Rabe.

When the 72-year old Ferdinand Porsche returned to Gmünd from French internment, he praised the completed plans: "I would not have altered a single screw."

Neverthless, completely unforeseen problems arose as the project was realized in Turin. Translation problems, unresolved detail questions, a particularly high percentage of self-produced components, and the first financial restrictions delayed its completion.

112■1

112■2

112■1 113■1

The low-mounted engine and the driver together formed the ideal unit for a suitably low center of gravity. The ribbed supercharger housings can be seen clearly, as can the the elongated five-speed transmission that is located behind the engine and also has cooling ribs

112■2

In the right frame outrigger we made our find: CIS-001, the number that the Argentinian customs officials were not to see

114 ■ 2

114 ■ 1

114 ■ 1
Like a stranded resident of mythical depths, the Cisitalia rests for a while on the Normandy coast

114 ■ 2
A glance at the cockpit reveals the no-compromise engineering, and the way it crowds in on the driver

115 ■ 1
Gentle melancholy surrounds the car. It's monstrous sound is lost to the world

114

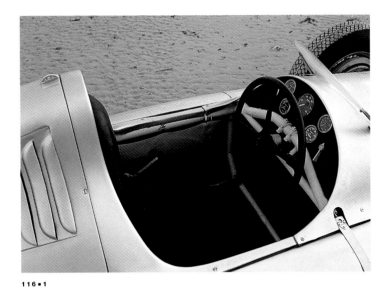

116 ∎ 1

116 ∎ 2

By the end of 1948, Cisitalia was financially ruined. Nevertheless, Dusio would not loosen his iron grip on the project and succeeded in nearly completing one of two cars. (Car number two was little more than a crate full of spare parts.)

Dusio's contact with General Peron fostered the hope that ongoing development of the car might take place in Argentinia, but the project ran aground completely as soon as the car reached Buenos Aires. The lifeline to the designers had been cut off, and the Type 360 was in danger of being forgotten, only to become the victim of unsuccessful attempts at recuscitation.

Beginning in 1952, the Grand Prix rules prohibited the use of mechanically supercharged engines, so plans were made to save Argentina's motor sport glory by at least setting up a new South American speed record. The GP pilot, Clemar Bucci, was selected to take the car down the airport highway, which was closed for the occassion, but due to a lack of suitable temperatures, spark plugs and fuel, the engine never

reached its true form and only propelled the car up to a disappointing average speed of 233 km/h (145 mph) – though this was fast enough for the record.)

The attempt was made with rear-wheel drive, since front tires of the correct size were not available and it was therefore not possible to establish the correct transmission ratio.

After intensive support from the Buenos Aires Institute of Technology, enough confidence was built up to enter the car for a non-formula race in 1953 at the Buenos Aires Autodrom.

The first test lap proved that Bucci was not able to master the gear shift. Felice Bonetto, the old Alfa, Maserati and Lancia pioneer, drove the next lap, but returned followed by a trail of smoke: dramatic oil loss, probably a split line. The car was taken out of the practice session.

Back to the test rig. There, in a magic moment under clinical conditions, the engine reached 385 hp at 9,000 rpm. Never-

116 ∎ 1

The cockpit reveals naked elements of the chrome-molybdenum frame. Next to the seat the gear lever can be seen clearly, which (a good idea in view of the lack of space) worked like a motorcycle shift

116 ∎ 2

The four-wheel hydraulic brakes adhered to Porsche's principle of outstandingly high retardation rates. Each drum contained four shoes, and an air scoop cooled the brake when the car was in motion. The handbrake too was hydraulically actuated

theless, possibly because the mixture was too lean, one or two pistons burned out. The complicated engine was dismantled, re-equipped with spare pistons, reassembled, and then dismantled again after it was discovered that a few small parts were left over. It never completely recovered from this process, and burned out again in later tests. In the end, the car was jacked up and offered for sale.

An entreprising American was found who wanted to put a Chevrolet engine in the car and enter it in dragster races.

Yet he too underestimated the problems and his interest waned enough to allow a crafty Hungarian, Anton von Döry, who owned a Porsche and NSU dealership in Buenos Aires, to succeed in shipping the car back to Germany, after bringing it through customs as a Porsche RSK. (This was a story in itself, involving a flooded boat house, a rescuing Unimog, and other activities under cover of darkness.) Since then the most adventurous GP car of all times has been kept in the Porsche Museum in Stuttgart.

Later, the second car also turned up in a garage near Turin and was restored for an American collector (or more accurately, was built up for the first time). This was achieved with the aid of the original plans which were available on microfilm. The engine, at least, had already been put together.

After the death of the American owner, an English racing-car owner acquired the car, which can be seen today in the Donington Grand Prix Collection, though without its crankshaft, the famous Hirth design with seven roller bearings.

Here are a few more informative tidbits to round the story off: The engine weighed 145 kg (320 lb), the dry sump lubrication (two suction pumps, one pressure pump) had to handle 25 liters of oil. The two pairs of double overhead camshafts were driven by vertical shafts. Two Weber downdraft carburetors supplied the mixture, which was compressed to 9.2:1. Maximum torque of 270 Nm (199 lb.ft) was reached at 6,000 rpm, the alleged peak output of 450 bhp at 10,500 rpm.

Finally – count along – the firing order: 1, 10, 5, 7, 3, 11, 6, 9, 2, 12, 4, 8. Are they all there?

Grand Prix Victory with Eight Cylinders, or: An Engine's Eternal Life

by Helmut Zwickl

AT THE "FESTIVAL OF SPEED" IN GOODWOOD, I was allowed to drive that Porsche Formula 1 race car with which Dan Gurney won the French Grand Prix in 1962.

It is a ride on top of the gas tank, which, artfully soldered, shapes itself around your body like a life jacket. The tank's thin aluminum skin contains 145 liters of fuel when the main and additional tanks are full. The tubular frame is rather like a birdcage. The battery is flanged on at a point next to your clutch foot.

Whereas Dan Gurney cut through the wind with his entire upper body, I was deep within the cage, and when I look at the pictures of Gurney in the cockpit, I am bound to reach the conclusion that the driver's size and weight was obviously not yet a decisive factor. Nowadays, for some race tracks, the computer spits out how many tenths of a second will be wasted for every 10 kilograms (22 pounds).

The eight-cylinder engine, which breathes through Weber carburetors, does not really kick in until it reaches 6,000 rpm. Below this level it wheezes asthmatically and powerlessly, and it is not until between 6,000 and 8,000 revolutions are displayed that a power peak is attained. This peak arrives as unexpectedly as toothpaste squirting out of the tube.

I enjoyed this alarming squirt on the short straights of Lord March's park, which is really nothing more than a narrow, paved road through the woods, enveloped by bushes and trees that turn it into a green tunnel. It resembles a section of the old Nürburg Ring, where Dan Gurney drove 8:47.2 and took pole position for the 1962 German Grand Prix.

Given today's safety-mindedness, which has been formed by technology and by the will to survive, driving this car to its limit might seem inconceivable.

What distinguished this Type 804 is the fact that the race car, with its eight-cylinder horizontally opposed enginee, gainfully employed only for this one season in 1962, somehow took out a lease on eternal life. It was milked for everything it had until 1968, by which time its two liters developed 272 bhp in hill climbs, and were even bored out to 2.2 liters.

At that time, the armaments race in motor racing was not quite as hectic as it is today. Nowadays they junk Formula 1 power units twice a season because they are rendered worthless by a new design.

In the late sommer of 1960, Dr. Hans Hönick and engineer Hans Mezger were given the green light for an eight cylinder engine, since it was clear that – in the 1.5-liter Formula 1 that had been in effect from 1961 – power output would climb to between 210 and 220 bhp, and designers would strive forengine speeds of 10,000 revs per minute.

Like the four-cylinder engine, the eight-cylinder version had double overhead camshafts for each cylinder bank, and the camshaft drive by vertical shafts was also adopted. The crankshaft runs in nine main bearings, the valves are actuated by cam followers. Cooling air was supplied by an axial fan positioned horizontally above the crankcase and driven from the upper intermediate shaft via a pair of bevel gears. At an engine speed of 10,000 rpm the fan runs at 9,200 rpm and delivers 1,400 liters per second, at a price of nine brake horsepower. The crankcase was made of cast magnesium.

804

119•1

*1961 was the year in which
Porsche's eight-cylinder Grand Prix
cars saw the light of day;
they scored second places
in Reims, in Italy and in the USA
during their first season*

SINGLE-SEATERS

Type 804 Formula 1 racing car

120 ▪ 1

Sitting inside this cockpit is like a riding on the fuel tank, which – artfully soldered – surrounds the driver's body like a lifejacket.

121 ▪ 1

Four overhead camshafts driven by vertical shafts, operate the eight-cylinder horizontally opposed engine's two valves per cylinder

121 ▪ 1

122 ■ 2

*The first Grand Prix successes
for the 804 came in July 1962:
Dan Gurney won the French
Grand Prix in Rouen with
a one-lap lead over the
South African driver
Tony Maggs in a Cooper*

122 ■ 1

*Dan Gurney, the driver associated
with most of the Porsche 804's
successes, judged the engine's
performance characteristic as
follows: "It was down on
mid-range power, and so it needed
a six-speed gearbox to keep the
engine running at the correct revs"*

In a descriptive article, Hans Mezger wrote: "One hindrance to quick development was the fact that many components had to be produced outside the company, and since the economy was booming, delivery periods were often too long. One example is the crankshaft, for which a forging die had to be made; it was not finished until nine months after it was ordered ..."

When run on the testing rig around Christmas time in 1960, the 1.5-liter version's power output was disappointing, failing to reach even180 bhp.

Not until the next winter was the power curve slowly coaxed up to the point where competitiveness was to be found: hemispherical combustion chambers and a change in the valve angle made new cylinder heads necessary, and merely by changing to titanium conrods 12 bhp were gained.

Later, Dan Gurney was able to make comparisons with the Brabham-Climax V-8, which put him in a position to offer a qualified assessment of Porsche's eight-cylinder engine: "There was a lack of power in the medium speed range, which is why a six-speed transmission was necessary to keep the engine turning over at the right speed."

The power curve bears out what Gurney remembered:

At 6,000 revs, there was only 120 bhp available, at 6,500 there was 138 bhp, at 7,000 barely 150 bhp, at 8,000 a solid 175 bhp, and at 9,000 nearly 190 bhp.

The engine was complicated and voluminous, and was not easy to tuck away in the steel tubular space frame, which weighed 38 kg (84 lb). The 0.8 mm (0.03 in) thick aluminum body, was later replaced by fiber-glass reinforced plastic.

A pump was used to transfer fuel from the main fuel tank to the nose tank and maintain the correct weight distribution (48 percent front, 52 percent rear) during races. The disc brakes, used for the first time, were an in-house product.

The 1962 Formula 1 World Championship did not begin until May, in Zandvoort. Ferry Porsche was far from confident: with the new formula 1 the company was taking the chance of damaging the marque's outstanding aura. It was not until practice on the Friday that he gave his blessing for the 804's racing debut in the Dutch Grand Prix .

Dan Gurney was in eighth position on the starting grid, 2.2 seconds behind the fastest driver in practice, John Surtees in a Lola, with the new Climax V8 engine at the rear.

The eight-cylinder Porsche's debut on Mai 20, 1962, took place somewhat in the shadow of the new Lotus 25. Colin Chapman had achieved a quantum leap forward with the pencil-thin sheet steel box chassis of this Lotus. Back then, the designers had freedoms that no longer exist today.

Gurney's gearshift lever broke first, then the driveline failed. Driving the second 804, Jo Bonnier took seventh place, with Carel de Beaufort finishing ahead of him in the old Formula 2 four-cylinder Porsche.

Ferry Porsche's fears thus turned out to be well founded, and as a result he took Monaco off the schedule. Nevertheless, Gurney succeeded at the last minute in gaining permission to start, and promptly became the innocent victim of a mass collision. Bonnier managed fifth place in the four-cylinder car.

Porsche decided not to participate in the Belgium Grand Prix, in order to check off a long list of improvements at the Nürburgring. For the front suspension, the young engineer Peter Falk designed additional longitudinal links since the suspension shook during braking. The seat was tilted back slightly – in the Lotus-25 Jim Clark lay flat as if on a deck chair. The tubular frame was made more rigid, the rear track widened by 5 centimeters (almost two inches), Bilstein shock absorbers replaced those from Koni. After Helmut Bott's chassis modifications and an 8:44.4 lap by Gurney, Ferry Porsche approved his team's trip to the French Grand Prix.

In Rouen, Gurney – who was suffering from angina – lined the car up behind Clark, Graham Hill, Bruce McLaren, Brabham and Surtees in the sixth starting position; he was just 1.7 seconds behind Clark. The competitors were no longer so far apart, and Ferrari was not at the start.

Gurney was sixth on the starting line and first to take the checkered flag. While in the lead, Clark and Hill had worn each other down tactically. The Scotsman dropped out due to defective suspension; on Hill's BRM the throttle linkage was defective.

Yet it was not this victory in the French Grand Prix that Gurney considered his best race in the 804, "but the Nürburg Ring, where it was raining, the battery cable came loose and I had to fight harder than ever before" – finishing third behind Hill and Surtees, just 4.3 seconds slower than the winner.

In the World Championship, Dan Gurney, who went on to become a cult figure in the American racing scene, ended up fifth behind World Champion Graham Hill, Clark, McLaren, and Surtees.

Once the year was over, the 804 became a museum item.

From sports car and GT races it was possible to derive invaluable know-how for the series production cars, whereas Formula 1 was not only expensive but led to a duplication of development effort.

The experienced gained by high-wire artist does nothing for pedestrians on the sidewalk.

And so Porsche withdrew from Formula 1.

125 ▪ 1
By the end of 1962 Porsche's Formula 1 outing was at an end for the time being. The main reason was that technical development involved spending disproportionate sums of money, but was only transferable to series production cars to a limited extent

By Heinz Prüller

Power, Professionals, Perfection

The TAG Turbo and the second Formula 1 era:
1983 to 1987

THE MCLAREN-TAG TURBO engine "made by Porsche" was the greatest thing that Formula 1 experienced in its most stormy phase: with 25 Grand Prix victories and three world championship titles, it was the most successful German racing engine in Formula 1 history. It set the standards in the turbo era, and amazed everyone – perhaps even more through its longevity as through its series of victories.

In the high-tech war that rages in the extremely fast-moving world of Formula 1, nobody solved the time problem better than Porsche.

The gigantic project was financed by Mansour Ojjeh's "Technique d'Avant Garde" (TAG) with five to ten million dollars a year – nobody can say today just exactly how much it was.

"But the people who did it were all pure-bred engineers from Porsche," recalls Niki Lauda, Porsche's first Formula 1 World Champion and still grateful today. "It was a really magnificent challenge. And the engine turned into a winner in no time at all – truly unique. It's probably my very best memory of Germany !"

The man who today is a "Piccolo Commendatore" had just returned in time from his first early retirement (Montreal, 1979). At first he was "anti-turbo," but that lost its appeal very quickly: "When your naturally aspirated engine has up to 160 bhp less that the turbocharged engines, racing becomes pointless."

Naturally, Hans Mezger knew this too. In his younger days, he had played in a student band, and now it was time to compose his masterpiece, which Porsche developed for McLaren: the 1.5-liter, six-cylinder, V-engine with an included angle of 80 degrees between the cylinder banks – the distinctive feature of this technlogical miracle, which Honda later copied shamelessly.

Why 80 degrees, Mr. Mezger?

"Having 80 degrees was really unusual, but we made the decision because the engine ran particularly smoothly."

Both of these turbo rockets, the Porsche and the Honda, were ready for the track simultaneously in 1983. Yet five years later, as the Japanese car took its first driver's world championship title, the McLaren-Porsches driven by Niki Lauda and Alain Prost had already won their third world championship title!

Anatomy of a super engine: Hans Mezger – begining in October 1981 – designed the cube-shaped engine originally for a wing car. When these were banned from the track, the small, compact engine proved to be even more suitable, since McLaren designer John Barnard clung reverently to the extreme "bottleneck principle": "The tail has to look like a Coke bottle."

The first bench tests were held in December 1982. Roland Kussmaul was at the wheel for the first test drives in Weissach. And in July 1983, Lauda drove his first laps in Silverstone. Niki's contract stated that he was allowed to be the first to drive all the important tests. So at first , John Watson just looked on and held the stopwatch. The experimental chassis – the McLaren MP 4, driven from 1981 on by Andrea de Cesaris – was now a rolling laboratory. The biggest challenge for drivers and engineers now began.

A glance in the rear-view mirror?

Hans Mezger explains: "The turbo is called turbo, because it uses exhaust-driven turbochargers – two to be exact, one on each side. The turbocharger has a turbine section and a compressor section. The turbine is driven by the exhaust gas, which enters from the three cylinders in each block of the vee engine. The turbine then drives the-compressor, which draws in air and compresses it. This heats up the air, and so it is passed through a charge-air intercooler. From there it is reaches the cylinders as combustion air."

The program was hot in every way.

Porsche mastered the technical problems with the same sensational speed as Lauda met the driving challenges: "Of course, full power is not available until the boost pressure builds up – and that takes time."

The famous "turbo lag" effect: "You brake when you come to a corner, but you step on the gas again a good distance before the actual curve – because it takes a second or two for the pressure to build up. Then you must be at the right point in the curve; you have full power, and you pull through. But I learned the technique just as quickly as my colleagues from Ferrari and Brabham …"

When Lauda makes a comparison with competitors, he knows: "There, the turbo engines flew apart after just a few laps. But our TAG turbo ran for 650 kilometers without the slightest problem." And another thing that made Lauda happy: "When you start up the Cosworth engine it always has this annoying vibration that tickles your back and your kidneys throughout the entire Grand Prix. The nice thing about the TAG turbo was that it was quieter, it didn't vibrate, and it didn't tickle you."

For a year, McLaren had an exclusive on the engine. Mansour Ojjeh was already dreaming of the day when there would be "an entire field of starters all with TAG turbos" – a dream which remained an illusion.

When the McLaren-Porsche "rocket" was finished, Ron Dennis in Zuffenhausen built up something like a "Berlin Wall": No one was allowed as much as a glance at the new car.

But there was something no one knew. Lauda has kept it to himself until now: No one knew that he became world champion with cunning and deception, blackmail of the most charming kind, and that the entire sensational series of early victories was owed to a Lauda trick.

McLaren did not want to run the turbo until 1984, but Lauda protested strongly: "We all know how long it takes to develop an engine like this. 1983 is nearly over. Let's use the rest of the Grands Prix for testing – so that we can make a run for the title right from the start in 1984." John Barnard, accustomed to delivering perfect cars, but always slightly ater than planned, refused categorically: "We're not going to run it until 1984, period!"

But then Lauda made use of his direct connection to Marlboro – a sponsor providing millions: "If Dennis and Barnard really don't want to deliver the turbo until 1984, you guys don't have to pay them as much for 1983 …"

Money is always effective in Formula 1. Ultimatums have their effect too: in Zandvoort, in late summer, the car was ready and waiting in the pits, and much admired: despite having two turbochargers, two intercoolers, and two waste gates, it was no heavier than a naturally aspirated engine – which does not need any of this extra equipment.

Those early entries were very, very important: the team established that the brakes and wings were two small, and that the cooling did not work properly – all of which was modified rapidly. "We already had 700 brake horsepower back then," recalls Ralf Hahn, who was in charge of testing and race meetings, and returned to Formula 1 in 1997 with Minardi after his Porsche and Ferrari career. "That was two hundred more than the naturally aspirated Cosworth engines."

129■1

129■2

The first engine had a compression ratio of 6.9 to 1, but by Kyalami it was already up to 7.2. The boost pressure then was 3.1 bar.

"But we didn't exploit the scope of the engine management system to the full. Fuel consumption was no problem – in 1983 you were still allowed to refuel" – later there was a period when this was not permitted. Today, however, it has long since been introduced again: out of necessity.

In 1983, the McLaren-Porsches did not see the checkered flag at the finish line. Barnard enlarged the radiators for each race, but the oversized brakes made Lauda and Watson jump on them 150 meters too early, after which it took a correspondingly long time to coax the engine back up to speed. In the world championship final in Kyalami, Lauda had the brakes under control for the first time – and won just like that! Since Alain Prost's turbocharger blew up in South Africa, Nelson Piquet became the first turbo world champion in the Brabham-BMW, but it was clear to everyone: From 1984 on, it would be McLaren-Porsche's turn. With Lauda, or ...? John Watson gambled too long for higher stakes. He wanted as much money as Lauda, but overlooked the fact that Prost was no longer on such good terms with Renault – and suddenly the Frenchman was free for McLaren!

"The fastest team-mate I ever had, and my greatest opponent in the battle for the world championship." Right away, Lauda corrected his strategy: "I didn't want to take a murderous risk on the qualifying laps with souped-up charge pressure – I left the pole-position laps to Prost and concentrated on getting my car ready for the race."

Turning the handwheel offered the drivers another tactical variation: higher boost pressure meant more horsepower, but it also went through more fuel. In Weissach, the compression ratio was increased to 7.8, the electronics were now much more refined, and above all, there was sequential fuel injection: no longer all at once for the entire cylinder bank, but timed separately for each each cylinder.

The Porsche engine was never thirsty: after Prost won his first race with Porsche in 1984 in Rio, the McLaren mechanics pumped 20 liters out of the tanks after the finish flag had been waved! But nobody's perfect: in Kyalami the Motronic's main plug fell off after the warm-up, whereupon it was secured with plastic tape. Simultaneously, Prost's fuel pump froze up due to the specially cooled fuel, which meant that the Frenchmean had to start from the pits. A typical example of just how close together triumph and defeat can be in Formula 1.

Lauda led from start to finish, but was

surprised by signals from the pits: "Prost P 2." His team-mate, after devouring the entire field, had stormed his way up to second place: The first double victory for the turbo from McLaren and TAG.

In 1984, the red & white rockets raced from victory to victory: Prost won seven times, Lauda five.

Here is how the sensational inner-team duel for the world championship title developed after Rio and Kyalami: in Imola: Prost first; Lauda: engine damage.

In Dijon: Lauda first. He had to "drive like a wild man to catch the leader Tambay twice after pit stops. Ron Dennis had delayed the pit stop for such a long time" – but Prost only took 7th place.

Monte Carlo: Prost finishes ahead of Ayrton Senna and the superb Stefan Bellof, as the race was terminated due to rain; but Lauda slipped up at the Casino: "First the water gets into your helmet, then into your brain, and then you start to spin."

Montreal: Lauda second, Prost third.

Detroit: Prost fourth, Lauda out due to a defective electrical system.

Dallas: Lauda and Prost both crashed against the wall.

Brands Hatch: Lauda first, Prost retired with transmission damage.

Hockenheim: Prost first, Lauda second.

Zeltweg: Lauda first, but with his heart pounding: the transmission was completely shot just before the end. "I just kept rolling along slowly, because I wanted to save myself the long walk back to the pits, but Piquet thought it was just tactics, and didn't attack," a fact which amazes Lauda to this day. Prost slipped on oil and slammed into the guard rails.

Zandvoort: Prost first, Lauda second – the team mate had struck back.

Monza: Lauda first, Prost suffered engine damage.

Nürburg Ring: Of all days, it was Professor Ferry Porsche's 75th birthday as Lauda had a rear wheel roll over his foot during testing in the Eifel, which caused alarm on German television: "The World Championship has been decided – Lauda has broken his leg." Prost won again, but Lauda salvaged fourth place.

And then came the Estoril photo finish. Just before the world championship final, Hans Mezger came to my TV studio in Vienna with a TAG turbo engine, and with the cameras rolling Lauda pleaded with the designer: "Hans, please – do everything you can to make sure the engine holds together!" The situation was clear: If Prost wins, Lauda definitely has to take second place. The sensational final to determine who would become Porsche's first Formula 1 world champion, fascinated millions.

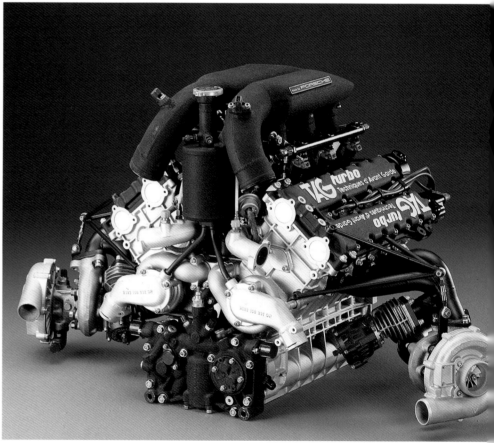

130•1

Up front, Prost stormed away. Lauda was wedged in at 11th place, fought madly, drove the best race of his life, but nearly lost hope of getting to the front. He didn't know why until later: the left turbocharger was not working – the blades were torn off, the oil pump broken – not Porsche's fault.

Yet Lauda was still able to battle his way to second place, coaxing the McLaren-Porsche along in the last laps: "Come on, you crazy car, make it to the finish!" His fear that the fuel might not last was unfounded. He drove the last laps as though in a trance: 13 seconds separated the McLaren-Porsches at the finish, the fourth double victory of the year.

Formula 1 had the champion it had hoped for (by half a point) – and the 113.5 points in the manufacturers' world championship remained the world record for a long time.

Porsche rejoiced with Lauda, McLaren laughed and cried with Prost: seven victories in one season and still not champion. "Don't worry about it," Niki comforted the unhappy Frenchman while they were still standing on the victory paltform, "next year you'll be the world champion, and I'll be helping you." Enough to dry Alain's tears

The world championship celebration in the "Coconut" disco was long and turbulent. Even nutrition and fitness guru Willi Dungl made – as English news-

papers reported in amazement – "*a sensational guest appearance as a whisky drinker…*"

McLaren-Porsche performance stayed superb in 1985 as well: The cars' new-generation Bosch Motronic system had four (instead of two) maps and electronic charge-air control. The drivers often needed to increase boost pressure in a two-car contest, but to save fuel, had to lower it again later. Normal racing pressure was 3.3 bar. In qualification practice, this went up to 3.8 bar. Power output during the race was 800 bhp.

There was a premiere in the middle of the 1985 season, at the French Grand Prix in Le Castellet: symmetrical turbochargers from Kühnle, Kopp und Kausch instead of two rotating in the same direction (to the right). "We also tested Garrett, but we couldn't find a clear edge. And the 120 kilometers from Zuffenhausen to Frankental are more favorable than the journey from the USA."

In 1985, as predicted, Prost became a masterful world champion, with triumphs in Rio, Monte Carlo, Silverstone, Zeltweg, and Monza. Lauda defeated his team-mate only once (in Zandvoort), but often dropped out due to vibration damaging the control unit and alternator. Then he handed over the cockpit to the "Flying Finn," Keke

Rosberg, who at the end of his career "definitely wanted to see how the McLaren-Porsche works."

By 1985, fuel cooling was forbidden. In 1986, tank capacity was reduced to 195 liters (51.5 US gallons). After disturbing knock and other noises at the beginning, Porsche tested other types of fuel in cooperation with Shell and began to use them. Compression was increased to 8.0; the 3.4 bar racing boost yielded 850 bhp; during the qualifying laps, Prost and Rosberg drove at 4.2 bar.

The third Motronic generation was received with pleasure. A small memory began storing data for engine parameters. And the ingenious John Barnard moved the chargers inward in order to exploit the ram effect.

In Hockenheim, people were nervous about Prost and Rosberg, who ran out of fuel on the last lap. The McLaren system: cockpit displays of the fuel still in the tank and the number of laps still to be driven, which the drivers compared with the pit display: So they knew whether they were on the positive or the negative side. Alain and Keke missed out by just one percent …

Prost defended his world championship title with four victories in Imola, Monte Carlo, Zeltweg, and Monza, but there too, hearts were pounding: In the final in Adelaide, Nigel Mansell had his eyes on the title when a rear tire exploded while he was traveling at 320 km/h (199 mph). Prost, cleverly, had already changed tires, and beat Nelson Piquet by four seconds in the sprint to the finishing line.

Porsche was world champion for the third time in succession! "I don't want to claim that our engine is the best. But I cannot accept other people saying that other engines were better!" says Ralf Hahn defensively.

More and more, Grand Prix races were being decided on fuel. "Those with better fuel consumption can run longer with more power," was the battle cry for the 1987 season, with 900 bhp, 3.5 bar boost, and a compression of 8.7.
Of all the drivers, Prost had the lowest material wear, used the least tire rubber, brake pads, and fuel. Alain and his new team-mate Stefan Johansson were able to make the fuel-air mixture leaner from the cockpit (three positions). But Prost never changed the setting! He always drove on the rich side. More internal cooling, less risk.
It was not until his fuel display broke in Spa that Prost radioed the pits to ask: "How much fuel is Stefan using?"

The engine speed climbed steadily from 11,200 rpm in 1983 to 12,600 rpm for a short time, then all the way up to 13,000 rpm. Data recording became more and more sophisticated. And in Mexico in 1987, the radio link was introduced "because at Porsche, we had promised we would do that too." The transmitter was located in the footwell, the receiver was on the pit wall.
In 1987, the famous "penny defect" cost Prost, McLaren, and Porsche their fourth world championship title in a row: a torn V-belt in Imola and Monza. The reason was discovered by high-frequency, strobosopic cameras on a test rig set up just for this purpose.
The result was the "twin belt." It solved a second petty problem: in 1985, Porsche had already replaced the standard electrical plugs with military plugs. "Without them, our wiring harness would have gotten thicker and thicker, and been impossible to install."

The long good-bye had already begun during the 1987 season. In late summer, the separation became final. Prost forced a world-record triumph in Estoril: His 28th Grand Prix victory, with which he surpassed Jackie Stewart's longstanding record (27) before retiring for good in 1994 with 51 victories, ten more than Senna.

In Portugal, Prost was happy: "I'm glad I was able to break the record with the Germans. Now I don't even want to think about my chances of winning the world championship any more. I just want to be happy, all night, all week – and until the world championship final in Adelaide."

Four days before the final race, in Adelaide, Ron Dennis invited the Porsche crew out for dinner: "Project Supporter" Ralf Hahn, data transmission engineer Wolfgang Steck, workshop group foreman Gerhard Küchle, and mechanic Lothar Feucht.
In his address "Mr. McLaren" said: "Thank you for your cooperation, which – with three world championship titles – could hardly have been more successful, but both sides now have reasons for ending this cooperation."
Funeral sweetmeats, swansong, a short address for a long goodbye – or a requiem for a six-cylinder turbo?

Prost and Johansson were stopped in the 68th and last Porsche race by brake defects. With the famous rusty nail in the heart and a certain amount of melancholy, the Porsche crew left the Grand Prix circus.
This departure saddened Ralf Hahn more than the others, "because I'm convinced we would have been up front again in 1988 after the new 2.5 bar, 150-liter rule! With a good 650 bhp, which was more than the new naturally aspirated engines had back then."

The green lamp was out: ever since the engine died on Prost in Zeltweg it had reminded the Porsche drivers below 3,500 rpm of the changed ratio for the alternator . In Formula 1, that fascinating arena for advanced racing technology, a light also went out. The TAG turbo engines "made by Porsche" found their way into the museum – just as Alfred Neubauer symbolically covered up his Silver Arrows after Monza in 1955.

Will they ever come back? Today, the 150 TAG turbo engines are in mothballs at McLaren. The plan to convert them into helicopter engines due to their sensationally low fuel consumption remained an illusion. McLaren never sold the German engines.

The end of the story, but the beginning of a legend. Later, much would be said on both sides: "It would have made more sense to continue to work together – but hindsight is always 20/20…"
Nobody can accuse the Germans of stubbornness. "On the contrary," recalls Hans Mezger, "We did additional things that were not in the contract – such as engine overhauls we never charged them for."

Ron Dennis is the only Formula 1 team manager to have worked together with the three big German engine makers. So it is only logical to ask him how they compare: "They're all different. Different cultures, different goals. For Porsche, we were paying customers, and Porsche was our engine maker – the relationship today is a partnership. For better or for worse, rich or poor," philosophizes Dennis.

And were they happier or less happy with Porsche from 1983 to 1987?
"All the periods of my life that have to do with racing victories make me happy. But that was a long time ago. I don't live in the past, I usually spend most of the time looking forward."

Ten years after the fact, Prost, on the other hand, offered a spontaneous answer to the question: "The McLaren-TAG turbo. Were those your nicest days in racing?": "My happiest days! Even 1984, despite losing the world championship by half a point."
A fascinating, exciting epoch, in the pits and the competitors' paddock. Princess Stephanie of Monaco was considered a big fan of Prost, and Lady Sarah (later known as "Fergie") was often seen in the McLaren pit.

A final word from Niki Lauda: "The decisive factor was that, with Porsche's support, I was able to force McLaren to enter its turbo car a year earlier. During the winter, all the weak points were weeded out, so we had the best, the most powerful, and the most durable engine from 1984 on – and drove them all into the ground." That was German speed.
Mansour Ojjeh, however, indirectly contributed to another racing marriage: In 1996, his American wife, Katie, was a witness at Gerhard Berger's marriage ceremony.

CRASH AT THE START, RACING VICTORIES WITH VW PARTS: FROM THE SPYDER TO FORMULA 2 AND INTO FORMULA 1

by Helmut Zwickl

THIS LETTER DATED AUGUST 4, 1960, which reached me in Vienna was addressed from Hemmersbach Castle, Horrem, District of Cologne, Germany and had been dispatched by none other than Count Wolfgang Berghe von Trips.

I had dared, as a completely unknown amateur journalist, to ask him four questions. Imagine: some nobody writes Michael Schumacher and torments him with a letter interview. I'm certain that such unreasonable requests land in the waste basket.

Wolfgang Trips was big-hearted enough to respond. He wrote me: "We drivers remain sceptical about the new Formula 1, since it replaced a formula that had not reached its technological limits, as this years' races clearly showed. It has become obvious that lowering the displacement limit from 2.5 to 1.5 liters was a sacrificed to a public (i.e. the press) that has an incorrect notion of the dangers of racing.

On the other hand, the new formula has, of course, also brought some interesting new elements in the engine and transmission area, but in view of the weight limit, there will hardly be any changes in the chassis area. I consider 450 kilograms (992 lb) to be a reasonable figure, but I can hardly believe that weight can influence the car's safety, as long as you cannot prove that your designer is wilfully negligent."

And his closing sentence: "We all think that the front-engined car as a low-displacement racing car can finally be written off."
Which brings us to the rear engine, rediscovered by Cooper and Lotus at the end of the 1950s. Based on Formula 2, they used it to bring about a revolution in Formula 1, and to reverse the polarity of the racing world towards a situation which had been Professor Porsche's technical credo in the days of his Auto Union racing cars.

This new German racing star, Wolfgang Trips, who drove together with Phil Hill, Richie Ginther, Cliff Allison, and Willy Mairesse in the 1960 Ferrari works team, and grew up with Porsche, was the central figure in the launch of the first, 100% pure Porsche Formel 2 racing car.

The road to this monoposto began in 1957 with a Spyder RS, that had a covered-over passenger seat. The cars weighed 530 kg (1,168 lb), which made them heavier than the Cooper Climax, but Edi Barth none the less won the Formula 2 class at the Nürburgring. In 1958 in Reims, Jean Behra, in a Porsche 1,500 RSK that had been modified to have the steering wheel in the middle and had an engine rated at 164 bhp, was up against 14 Coopers, three Lotuses, three Oscas, and the 182-bhp strong Ferrari. On the super-fast Reims circuit the streamlined RSK had an edge on the conventional single-seaters. Moreover, Behra drove just as daringly as ever. He stormed away from them all and took the checkered flag.

In the winter of 1958/59, Porsche made its first genuine single-seater. Count Trips drove the first test on the Nürburg Ring: 9:29 min. was a sensational time for the north loop.

Days later, the car went straight to the Monaco Grand Prix, where Formula 2 cars were also allowed to start. Four years after Mercedes, there was now a German car on the starting line once again in Monaco. Trips drove this works

135•1
1960 was "harvest time" for the Porsche Formula 2 single seater: numerous successes crowned by a three-fold triumph in Aintree, England, brought it the much sought-after "Coupe des Constructeurs," the inofficial Formula 2 world manufacturers' championship

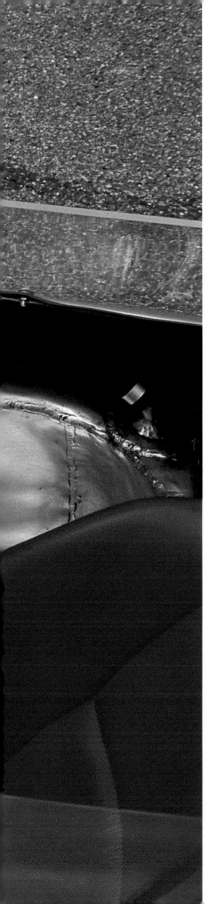

SINGLE-SEATERS
Formula 2 car with rear engine

136 ▪ 1

*A glance at the cockpit of
a pure-bred monoposto.
Its predecessors on the family
tree were the Spyder RS
and a 1500 RSK modified
to centre steering*

137 ▪ 1

*The engine concept was created
by Dr. Fuhrmann and Karl Rabe
and was developed in 1952/53.
The carburetor version of
the flat-four engine with its
four overhead camshafts
developed 165 bhp*

139 ▪ 1

In 1961, it was time for the 718/Formula 2 race car to bow out gracefully. Nevertheless, it retained its significance even after the season ended, since the modified single-seater provided Porsche with important experience for its entry into Formula 1

car. The Italian Maria-Teresa de Filipis was unable to qualify the car known as the "Behra-Porsche," which the Frenchman had developed at Colotti as a private project.

Trips slammed Porsche's Formula 2 unique creation against a wall in the second lap after sliding on the track, which according to Trips was "soapy with fuel that had spilled out of the cars' full tanks.

The Count was sharply criticized by the "Auto, Motor und Sport" reporter at that time, Günther Molter: "Trips was unfortunately given more responsibility than he was able to handle ... it would have been better to dig more deeply into the coffers and get a top-class driver to do the job."

The project was now a wreck, the 1959 season was a total loss, the sports-car entries had priority – but 1960 was harvest time!

With the Type 718, Porsche won the Formula 2 World Manufacturers' Championship title, thanks to points scored in the races in Syracuse, Brussels (Moss took second place), Aintree (one-two-three victory for Moss, Bonnier and Graham Hill), Pau and at the Nürburg Ring (where Bonnier won ahead of Trips).

Stirling Moss, in a midnight-blue Rob Walker Porsche, pulled off four victories from 9 Formula 2 starts: Aintree, Zeltweg, Cape Grand Prix in Killarney, and the South African GP in East London.

By making a gear-shift error in Aintree, Moss took the unfortunate engine up to 9,000 rpm, "but it didn't blink an eye." The only thing that bothered Stirling about the Porsche was the "imprecise six-speed gearshift," so he had a Maserati 250F Formula 1 shift gate installed.

1961, the first year of the 1.5-liter formula, proved to be a Ferrari season. Maranello had the most powerful engine, Phil Hill and Graf Trips duelled mercilessly for the title, and only Moss was able to humble them in Monaco and on the Nürburg Ring with his private Lotus. With its two-year-old car concept, Porsche had reached the end of the line in its ability to compete: incredibly, the front suspension crank arms were still from VW.

The air-cooled flat four engine that had been designed in 1952/53 by Dr. Fuhrmann and Karl Rabe – with 1.5 liters and 165 bhp on tap – had also reached a "sound barrier" that was nonetheless broken through with the aid of a fuel injection system from the Swiss engineer Michel May – but it came too late. The 180 bhp that the engine developed in Zandvoort in 1962 represented the end of the four-cylinder unit's career, but was just the beginning for the new eight-cylinder.

Nonetheless, in 1961, Dan Gurney took third place together with Moss in the World Championship, thanks to three second places (Reims, Monza, Watkins Glen) and one fifth place (Monaco).

The eight-cylinder engine was long overdue.

CHAPTER 6

Sports Stars

Sheer strength comes from engine size, they say, and then from turbocharging. The Porsche 917, with five liters and twelve cylinders, opened up new prospects beyond the 600-horsepower barrier. And then Porsche forced the pace by turbocharging this engine until its power curve climbed to regions in which even the kilowatts, let alone the horsepower, come in four figures.

In 1970, it was the Porsche 917 that fulfilled a long – and expensive – dream: overall victory in the Le Mans 24-hour race.

Complete with turbocharger, the 917 thereupon emigrated to America. With a good thousand horsepower on tap, it was so potent and so successful that the rules were changed to eliminate it after two championship wins.

917 – THE WINNING TYPE
Almost undriveable at first, Porsche's 12-cylinder car won a series of races in 1970

917/30
Unbeatable in two CanAm racing seasons

MOBY DICK
The Porsche 911 in absolute top form: 900 bhp!

956/962
With 14 wins in twenty years, this unforgettable sports car wrote history in Le Mans

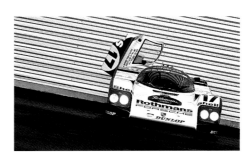

THE GUARD RAILS BEGAN TO VIBRATE, AND THERE WAS AN EERIE SILENCE IN THE COCKPIT

by Helmut Zwickl

917

WHEN YOU BREAK THE SOUND BARRIER in a fighter jet (as I found out in a Northrop F5F) not much happens inside: there is a short trembling followed by a deathly silence, and the needle on the air-speed indicator begins to shake.

In 1969, as Rolf Stommelen put his Porsche 917 on the afterburner, so to speak, on the long straights of Le Mans, there was also an "eerie stillness in the cockpit as the tachometer trembled its way up to 8,200 ..."

You don't hear that famous bang yourself, neither in the jet nor in the 917. Outside, of course, if a jet happens to break through the sound barrier, it leaves a trail of broken windows.

As Rolf Stommelen's 917 began to suck up the 5-kilometer straight like a hallway rug, I was standing at the right-hand bend in Hunaudières, and all of a sudden there was a singing in the air, such as you sometimes hear from telegraph wires, and simultaneously the guard rails began to vibrate; Porsche's projectile was disturbing a lot of air – acoustically as well.

At this moment a certain "sound barrier" was also broken through in Le Mans.

Stommelen arrived with a "vuuuow" and disappeared into the pine woods like a shooting star. No window panes broke as the result of this celestial phenomenon. There were no speed sensors in the car to transmit the top speed to the pits via telemetry, so the good old transmission graph had to do the job instead. As soon as Stommelen brought back his record of "8,200 in fifth," the variable for tire expansion hadto be added to it in order to determine the true top speed. It was between 350 and 355 km/h (217 - 221 mph).

Porsche, of course, already had an IBM computer on its home ground. The electronic brain had calculated a theoretical lap time of 3:25.76 minutes for the 917 in Le Mans, which Rolf promptly corrected to 3:22.9, representing an incredible average of 238.97 km/h (148.48 mph).

He had to lift off in the right-hand bend at Hunaudières, Stommelen confessed. Humming contentedly in its warm office,the computer had printed out 319 km/h (198 mph) for this bend, blissfully unaware that, for the 917 drivers, the Le Mans sound barrier was an adventure similar to the one that jet pilots once experienced as they battered themselves against the same barrier in the air. It all began three months before this epoch-making Le Mans lap.

On March 12, 1969 Porsche's "White Giant," the 917, was unveiled. There had been rumors about it for the previous six months. Its development period – just eight months – had been sensationally fast. With 4.5 liters and 12 cylinders (which supplied 580 bhp initially), Ferdinand Piëch wanted to reprogram Porsche towards overall race victories.

The role of a David who constantly gave Goliath a black eye was too small for him. In long-distance races, only overall victories mattered, nothing else. Porsche planned to turn the duel between Ford and Ferrari into a three-way battle, and no longer just win the junior class. "In May 1968," said Piëch, "the first sketches were drawn for the 917." In March 1969, production began, since 25 cars had to be built for homologation. Production, test programs, and racing involvement: back then, with strategists Piëch and Bott, Porsche began an unparalleled pro-

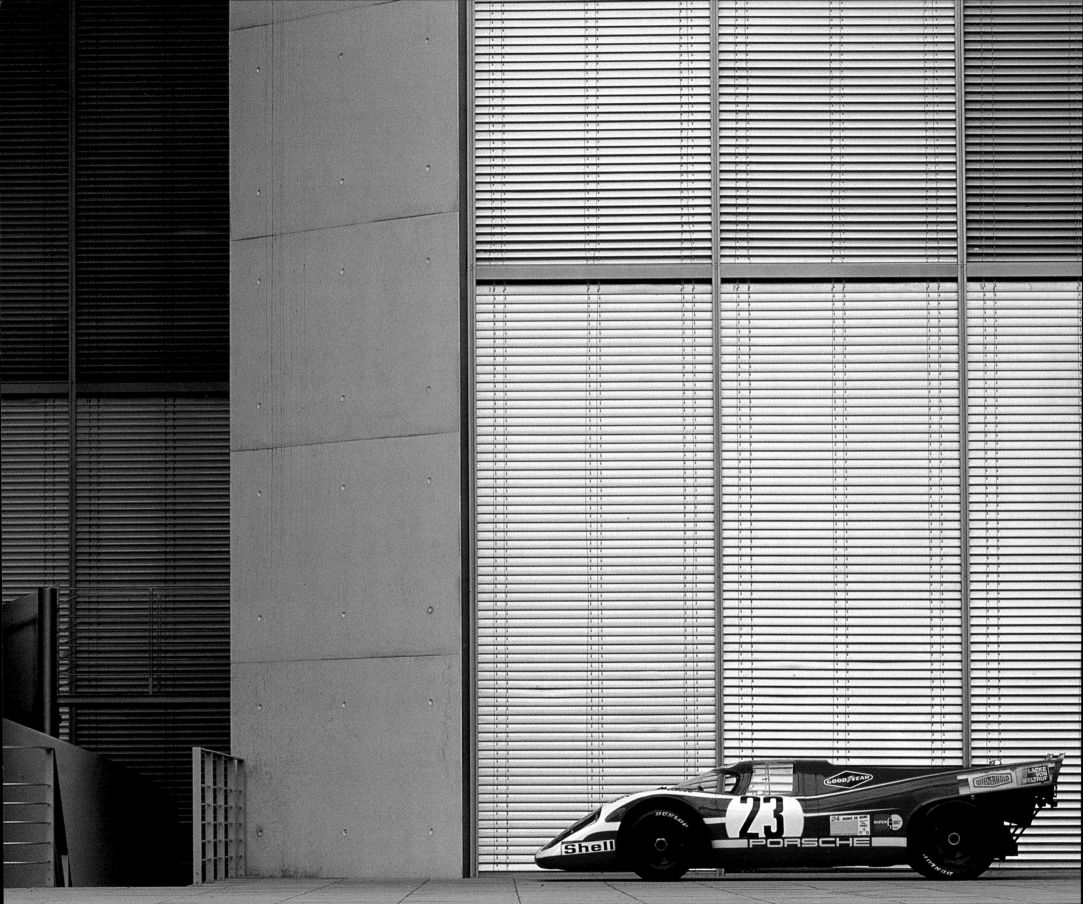

gram that even outshone the great days of the post-war Mercedes Silver Arrows 15 years previously. In the 917, the driver sat "with his eyes ten centimeters closer to the front axle than in the 908," Piëch was heard to say. Gerhard Mitter had some doubts: "I'm curious how it will be to drive this thing from such a forward seating position with this kind of power behind your back. In our hill-climb car, you also sit extremely far forward – but with 580 horsepower in a backpack as long as this – can it work?" It didn't work in the first season, anyway!

The super racer's technology looked like this: light aviation-grade aluminum space frame welded by a special method that took Porsche nearly a year to develop. Lightweight construction *über alles*. Even the gear lever knob was made of balsa wood. The Giant had right-hand drive. Engine specialist Hans Mezger designed the long crankshaft so that – as far as torsional vibrations were concerned – it was actually two short shafts. The drive was taken from a gearwheel located between the two center main bearings. The drive to the camshafts (two per cylinder bank) is also taken off at this point. Since the individual cylinders do not "box" with each other, the engine is referred to in engineering parlance as a 180-degree V-12. For its day, the engine was extremely compact, only 10 cm (3.9 inches) longer than the three-liter eight-cylinder engine. Gasoline injection is by double-row pump with twelve plungers. At 8,400 rpm, the cooling fan – driven at 0.89 times engine speed – delivers 2,400 liters of air per second, at a cost of 17 bhp in terms of power loss.

For Le Mans, the company already had 580 bhp at 8,400 rpm to tackle the Fords and the Ferraris, and the torque of 52 mkg at 6,800 rpm was a source of genuine pleasure.

The cost of materials alone for the most-powerful Porsche that had ever been built to that date were estimated at 220,000 German Marks, half of which was spent on the engine and transmission unit. It took approximately 200 hours of work to put the twelve-cylinder engine together. Since the selling price was set at 140,000 German Marks, the cars were sold at a loss.

"Who has driven the car so far?" Josef Siffert wanted to know as the 917 was unveiled at the Geneva Motor Show. "No-one," he was told. And the time soon came around when "no-one" wanted to drive the 917.

At the pre-practice session in Le Mans, Hans Herrmann thought that "the entire car would collapse during acceleration because of its sheer power. This turned out to be bearable, but it was true that at 300 km/h (186 mph), "the car became so unstable, that its suddenly started to snake. I didn't dare press the pedal to the floor ...," Hans reported to the technicians in the pits. The twelve-cylinder engine took such deep breaths that the inhalation casued the rear window to break.

Ferdinand Piëch wanted to see for himself just how powerful the 917 was. He wedged himself behind the steering wheel and drove the 917 over to the Porsche headquarters in Teloche.

"But in first gear," said his drivers with a grin.

The 917 was put through an extensive testing program. It was flogged around the rough-surface course in Weissach and subjected to endurance runs on the roller test rig with braking, shifting, and acceleration phases. By the beginning of May, the 4.5-liter engine had already stood up to three hours at full load, for forty percent of which time the engine had run at speeds between 8,000 and 8,600 rpm. The goal was 18 full-load hours.

In Spa-Francorchamps, Josef Siffert refused the 917, whereupon Gerhard Mitter volunteered to help: He was a fearless, ambitious fearless driver who loved the feeling of occupying the ejector seat. Unfortunately, he overrevved the engine on the starting lap.

According to the IBM computer, the 917 should have been four seconds faster than the 908 on the Nürburgring. In reality, it was 30 seconds slower. "This is because we are not yet achieving optimal lateral acceleration," explained engineer Helmut Bott, " It is a question of precise tuning and of the entire wheel kinematics."

It took a long time to find out what the problem really was, but it turned out to be the aerodynamics, causing the car to pre-

144 ▪ 1
*In May 1968, the first sketches were made for the 917.
In March 1969, production of the 25 cars required for type approval began. The body's supple outer skin clings to the lightweight aluminum space frame*

145 ▪ 1
According to Ferdinand Piëch, in the 917 the driver sat "with his eyes 10 centimeters closer to the front axle than in the 908"

147 ▪ 1
Winged monster: the Porsche 917. In the Le Mans prepractice session, the twelve-cylinder engine took such powerful, deep breaths that the rear window was pulled out and shattered

148 ■ 1

148 ■ 2

148 ■ 3

148 ■ 4

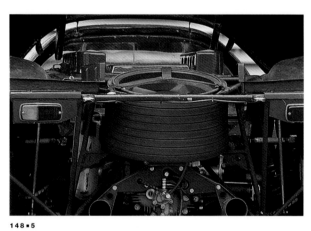

148 ■ 5

148 ■ 6

148 ■ 7

148 ■ 8

148 ■ 9

The 917, which sucked in the straights like a hallway rug, was – in every detail – the last word in automobile racing technology. Lightweight construction wherever you look. Even the gearshift knob was made of balsa wood. The value of the car's materials alone added up to 220,000 German Marks. The 25 models produced were sold (for a loss) at 140,000 German Marks. Porsche and its young designer Ferdinand Piëch wanted to win at any price

fer flying to a ground-based career. None of the works drivers was keen to act as a guinea-pig during experiments with the White Giant.

Race manager Rico Steinemann was sent out to find some drivers who were more willing. He found Dieter Quester and Hubert Hahne. After three laps Hahne drove a remarkable 8:38 min, and climbed out of the car somewhat intimidated: "What power! You never know if you have it in third or in fifth..." Dieter Quester admitted to being "scared."

But then came the command from Munich for the BMW works drivers: do not start in this race for Porsche!

Other professionals, David Piper and Frank Gardner, were found, drove the 917 (known internally as the "ulcer") in the 1,000-km (621-mile) in the race and took eighth place.

Before Le Mans, the front suspension kinematics were modified. During the evening practice runs it became clear that the 917s with movable rear wings (controlled mechanically by the suspension) had far superior directional stability and hugged the road much more closely in the fast curves than with the fixed rear wings that the senior CSI sports commission required. It proved possible to convince the CSI that this feature represented a safety improvement, and it authorised movable rear wings again for the race.

The 1969 Le Mans went into history as the "one-and-a-quarter-hours" race. It got off to a fatal start, was fascinating during the evening, gruelling and long-winded during the night, and murmured along sedately in the morning – Le Mans showing all of its aspects. But it was not until the last hour and fifteen minutes that it became what it had not been so far: a race.

Hans Herrmann was 41. No longer quite as fresh as the morning dew, but a mature individual, still fast, never risky, not a taskmaster for the car, but more of a virtuoso musician who gently caresses the strings of his instrument, a professor for long distances. 78 minutes before the close of the 24-hour race, he suddenly realized that he would have to drive faster than he

liked if he was to rescue something for Porsche. After two laps, the red warning light for the brakes lit up on the dashboard of his Porsche 908. That meant: a pad was worn through, he needed to make a pit stop on one of the next two laps.

Of course, Herrmann drove the entire last hour. At the beginning of the straights, in fourth and fifth gear, he was able to keep in the slipstream of the Ford GT40, then even pull out and pass. But since the engine was peaking 400 revs below its nominal maximum speed, Jacky Ickx usually pulled away again on the last part of the straight.

At 1:10 PM – it could have been a plot idea from a Hitchcock film – the battling Ickx-Herrmann duo ran up against the second of John Wyer's Fords, occupied by Ickx's teammate Mike Hailwood. Ickx made it past, Herrmann had to stay in line. "Two Porsches against a Ford would have made just as much out of the situation," Hans commented later. In Hailwood's slipstream, the 908 found their speed again, the revs climbing up over the 8,000 mark. Thus, unwittingly, it was Hailwood who pulled the Porsche back up close to Ickx. Twelve minutes before the end Hans still led across the start and finish line, "but I could not risk anything more with the brakes." With nothing but a damp patch in the bottom of the gas tank, but with a three-second lead, Jacky Ickx took the checkered flag with co-driver Jackie Oliver.

Porsche lost at Le Mans, but the Manufacturers' World Championship was won with the three-liter engine: In the 1969 season, Porsche became world champion thanks to a technical knock out. A year later, after winning the 24-hour Daytona race with Rodriguez/Kinnunen and Siffert/Redman as drivers, the 917 celebrated its own Thanksgiving Feast in Le Mans.

Porsche had moved mountains to pull off this first overall Le Mans victory. Attwood-Herrmann, the personified long-distance intelligentsia, scored the result that all had waited for so long .

For Herrmann, this was the high point of his almost 20-year career, which began at Porsche, and which he – in sparkling style – terminated with this victory.

Two Turbochargers Pump Power into a Displacement of 5.4 Liters

by Clauspeter Becker

917/30

HANS MEZGER, THE MASTER BUILDER of racing car engines at Porsche, loved to tell this story (as soon as enough years had gone by for him to be able to do so).

It was a cool morning, rich in oxygen, he reports, and the 5.4-liter 12-cylinder engine had behaved well on the test rig. "We wanted to give it one more quick performance check before we sent it by plane to Roger Penske in America." As Mezger explains what then happened, the boost pressure in his voice rises noticeably. "But when the engine had reached the rated speed and full load and we began to register its peak output, the needle kept jerking ahead – far beyond any of the values we had ever measured. For a few fractions of a second, the engine reached 1,450 bhp. This performance explosion proved later to have been caused by a defect: the boost pressure control had failed. Normally, no engine can survive anything like that, but afterwards, the 12-cylinder continued to run like a charm."

This made the 917/30's engine the most powerful unit ever used in a true racing car: The fact that today's racing trucks and dragsters are more powerful still is a fact we just have to accept (though naturally with an appropriate hint of disdain).

The natural superiority of the 917's 12-cylinder engine is one of those impressive achievements that Ferdinand Piëch has always demanded in his life-long striving for the ultimate. At that time, the rules of the sport supported this daring scheme, since they allowed sports cars to have a displacement of five instead of the previous three liters.

During the summer of 1968, the design of this flat, air-cooled power plant began to mature. At first glance the engine looks like two horizontally opposed, flat-six "boxers" joined together – underlined by the fact that the power take-off is at the middle of the long crankshaft and not from one end, as is usually the case.

Nevertheless, at heart this Porsche engine is not a true relative of the company's four, six, and eight cylinder horizontally opposed designs. On the crankshaft of this 12-cylinder engine the connecting rods of opposing pistons are not attached to two offset crankpins, but to a single shared pin. This simplification offers the advantage that the number of crankshaft main bearings can be reduced from 14 to eight, which reduces friction losses. It also eliminates the characteristic "boxing" action of each pair of pistons in a genuine horizontally opposed engine. For this reason, engineers consider this simplified design principle to be more closely related to the familiar V-engine. This fact may come as a surprise when we consider that the included angle between the cylinder banks is 180 degrees – and what could be less vee-like than that?

When the 12-cylinder began its career (with a swept volume of 4.5 liters, but still without a turbocharger), the engineers were looking for a power output of 560 bhp at 8,300 rpm. During development, however, the displacement increased to 5.4 liters and the output followed suit, rising to 660 bhp at 8,300 rpm.

Initially the Porsche 917 (built as a short production run of 35 cars) cost as much as a 911 with sport package costs

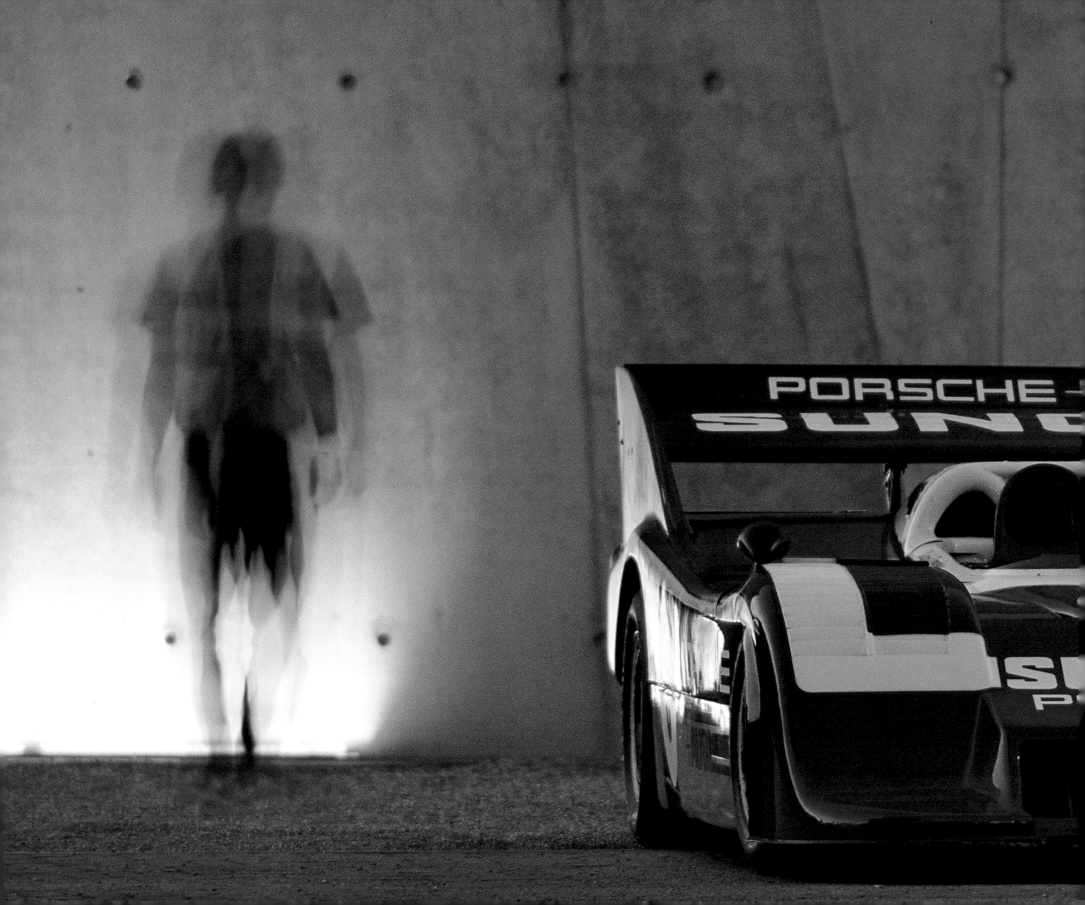

SPORTS STARS
Donohue & 1100 PS

153 ■ 1

*The turbo engine draws in cool air
for its 12 cylinders through a large
round hole in its hood. These 12
produce more than 1,100 bhp
and burn a liter of fuel per kilometer
(about six tenths of a mile)!*

152 ■ 1

*The low nose and powerful rear
wing create a downforce that
presses the CanAm Porsche
onto the road.
This increases aerodynamic drag
and means that a portion of the
car's power has to be sacrificed for
road grip*

153

154 ■ 1

154 ■ 2

154 ■ 3

154 ■ 4

154 ■ 1

The Porsche 917/30's safety tanks can hold up to 400 liters of aviation gasoline, sufficient for 400 kilometers (about 250 miles) at racing speeds

154 ■ 2

1,100 bhp and 1,100 Newton meters of torque reach the road through these rear tires, which are 370 millimeters (about 14.5 inches) wide – big stuff in 1973!

154 ■ 3

The 917/30 still had a classic tubular frame made of lightweight magnesium. It was not until later that Porsche switched to mono-coque technology, which at that time was in its infancy

154 ■ 4

In the cockpit, pure engineering surrounds the driver. The tacho-meter, which (except for the figures) shares its design with the 911, links the car to the production Porsches

155 ■ 1

The wheel caps on the wide 19-inch rear wheels have fan blades to cool the brakes.
To the left of the thick exhaust pipe is the waste gate, which controls charge-air pressure precisely according to the power demand

today: 140,000 German Marks. Despite this high price, drivers were "shocked" by the car's ride: the prototype is said to have behaved most unpleasantly. Much detail work was required to tame the car, but once this was done, the positive side of this raw power came to the forefront: there was no stopping the 917. It won wherever it wanted to, and in Europe finally relieved Porsche of the role of the underdog that was achieving surprising successes with inferior cars.

Neither the factory team nor the private entrants had to put up much of a fight on the road to victory: in 1969 the car was second in Le Mans, in 1970 it was finally victorious. It calmly made off with the World Manufacturers' Championship. In view of this, the end of the power race in Europe was impossible to prevent. The displacement limit for cars participating in the World Championship was reduced again.

As a result, Porsche planned its next series of successes for the area in which it was already selling the more cars than anywhere else: America. The CanAm series imposed few limits on "two-seater" sports cars, and seemed to offer the right challenge.

The cars that drove in this series belonged in the robust American low-tech category: sports cars with tubular steel space frames, powered by V8 engines of simple American provenance: 8.2 liters displacement, though with an aluminum block, a material seldom selected otherwise.

In 1971, with a non-turbocharged 917 Spyder, Jo Siffert had no chance of finishing well in the rumbustious "Jurassic Park" that was the CanAm series. In Weissach, however, Hans Mezger was working diligently on the next performance hike. Two methods of extracting more power were examined: one was more or less conventional, and attempted to move up to the next size category by adding four pots to yield a 16-cylinder engine, just like the engine that Ferdinand Porsche had designed for the Auto Union 40 years previously. This attempt to bring the past back to life was foiled by practical results from the test rig. At 850 bhp, the perform-

ance achieved on the testing rig by the more progressive alternative, a 12-cylinder engine with twin turbochargers, far exceeded the 655 bhp from its more complex colleague with four 4-cylinder blocks.

Roger Penske's team first entered a 917/10 in the 1972 CanAm series, with Marc Donahue as driver. After Marc was involved in an accident, George Follmer stood in for him – and ended the season in Riverside as champion.

Although the Porsche was far superior to all its competitors – McLaren, Lola, Shadow, and Ferrari – race engineer Norbert Singer remembers a few worries they had in the winter after the first CanAm season: "For one thing, we needed more stable handling for the high power. That is why we considered extending the wheel base beyond 2,300 millimeters

156 ▪ 1
Since all the Porsche 917/30's competitors got to see was this imposing tail, the American sports rules soon put an end to the power play of turbocharged engines with more than 1.000 bhp on tap. The Porsche was given the same sentence as many victors before and since: museum, for life

156 ▪ 1

(90.5-inches) for the first time in Porsche's history. In terms of top speed too, we would have liked to have been farther ahead of the McLaren."

The health cure took place on the Le Castellet race track in the South of France. For the chassis and suspension tests, the team took along an extension bridge that could be inserted into the magnesium space-frame tubes between the driver and the engine, to extend the wheelbase by 200 millimeters (7.87 inches).

After a test-drive program with the old, short wheelbase and the new, powerful 5.4-liter engine rated at 1,100 bhp, a lot of work remained for the late shift to do: the engine had to be removed; the chassis disassembled and the extension bridge put into place. The next test drive was performed in fantastic times, and Norbert Singer also had several other reasons to be happy: "Directional stability was greatly improved , turn-in was no less agile than before, and it was now much easier to control the car at the cornering limit. After this, the team began work on increasing the top speed.

Norbert Singer explains: "We knew just what to do after all the long-tail versions in the past, but we were not prepared for things to move so quickly, and had no finished parts with us." So they welded the auxiliary frames they needed from light-alloy tube. Aluminum sheets for the provisional body parts came from local metal suppliers. Singer describes the final design as a craftwork adventure: "We beat the parts into the desired shapes well as we could over a guide rail. We would never would have won a beauty contest for our work. But when everything was put on, it fitted. Afterwards, the 917/30 was considerably faster."

The American team worked hard to make sure that the cars looked good. Roger Penske's comment: "Porsche makes cars that are technically perfect, but the finish does not come up to my expectations. So I have them taken apart, the frame and all the unpainted parts polished and put back together very neatly."

The Porsches thus started their second Can-Am season looking suitably elegant and with a top speed of 385 kph (239 mph). The official power output was 1,100 bhp at 7,800 rpm. Torque was a scary 1,010 Newton meters at 6,400 rpm. With that much traction, a four-speed transmission was sufficient, with very wide gear teeth and extremely solid synchronizer assemblies. Since the engine's power made it possible to drift through nearly every curve, there was no need to install anything as commonplace as a differential.

The additional power and speed was sufficient to leave the fast McLaren with its 8.2-liter aluminum Chevy engine even further behind than previously. Marc Donohue won six of seven races in the 1973 CanAm series and became champion by a massive margin. In the final Championship listings, Porsche 917s took the first four places and also the sixth. Such clear superiority sealed the fate of the turbocharger and thus of Porsche's prospects in the CanAm series. The rules were changed, the turbo tigers had to go. American cars with roaring big block engines had things all to themselves again. In the shape of the Porsche 917/30, the worst gas-guzzlers of the day were banned from the track in 1973, the year of the first oil crisis. A turbo engine of this kind, tuned for racing, developed 1,000 to 1,100 bhp and easily burned a liter of aviation gas per kilometer. The 400-liter tank was usually empty after 400 kilometers (roughly 250 miles) or just less than two hours.

Two years later, in 1975, Marc Donohue again had an opportunity to show what a Porsche 917/30 could really do. In Talladega (Alabama), he drove fastest lap at an average speed of 355.85 kph (221.11 mph).

For its 20th anniversary, the Porsche 917/30 with Sunoco decor took another trip to the USA. Hans Joachim Stuck had the pleasure in driving it to victory in the Laguna Seca Classic Race. After tackling the twisty circuit with his usual gusto, Stuck revealed how much he regretted not having started to drive the CanAm 20 years early. "I've always said that a car needs at least a thousand horsepower to be really good and safe."

A Monster Slips
Through Gaps in the Law's Net

by Clauspeter Becker

935

EVEN YEARS LATER, you can sense the profound emotion when Swiss driver Manfred Schurti remembers "Moby Dick" and the 24-hour race in Le Mans: "At 366 kilometers an hour (227 mph) on the Mulsanne straight, there is only one thing you can do: Keep your foot bravely on the gas pedal."

This official measurement taken by the "Automobile Club de l'Ouest" confirms that the Porsche 935 "Moby Dick" is the fastest member of the hard-driving 911 family ever to take to the road. For it is still easy to see that this beast from the racing department is a Porsche 911.

Yet the path to this top form was not anything like as straight as the one in Mulsanne. Shortly before the finishing line, the creation of the ultimate 911 of the 1970's had to negotiate a slalom through various sections of motorsport law.

Things started in a straight-enough line. In the late 1970's, Porsche's model designations were still very correct: 924 meant the new four-cylinder model, and 928 was the logical designation for the more powerful model with eight cylinders. Among the potent 911's, code number 930 designates the standard Porsche Turbo, which proved to be extremely well suited to build upon. It turned up again under the name 934 as a near-series Group 4 competition car for special Grand Touring events. As a 935 it can be clearly identified as belonging to the wilder Group 5, the class for sports cars which much none the less reveal more than just coincidental similarities with production models. The 936 represents the culmination of all sporting character: a Group 6 sports prototype, an open racing car and no obligation whatsoever to the series production cars.

From 1976 on, it was possible for competition drivers to purchase the Porsche 934 and 935. The tamer 934 mobilized first 485 bhp, later 580 bhp from the three-liter displacement customary for the Turbo at that time. With this kind of power, the car, which weighed 1,150 kg (2535 lb), went rather well – and for 108,000 German Marks, was a bargain from today's perspective.

In those days, however, the 935 was considered the real tough guy. It was not just more expensive, but with two turbochargers and many other goodies it was a much more thoroughbred racer. The basic power output from the biturbo engine, which offered plenty of room for further development and was only reduced to 2,806 cc because of the motor-racing authority's rules, was estimated conservatively as 590 bhp.

The fact that there was more power available for the 1976 Manufacturers' World Championship was due largely to the so-called "steam wheel" with which the brave person at the wheel can raise the maximum boost pressure. In the "Grosses Buch der Porsche-Typen," authors Lothar Boschen and Jürgen Barth revealed the effect of this instrument with the simple formula: 0.1 more boost pressure adds 50 bhp.

With a suitable degree of boost, the Porsche 935 was world production car champion in its first season. Among the sports cars, the 936 Spyder with an open body and very similar power-train technology took the World Championship title for sports cars. In addition, Jacky Ickx and Gijs van Lennep won the Le Mans 24-hour race in the Spyder.

As is still the case today, these races were not only won

The Porsche 935 was nicknamed "Moby Dick" because of its figure. As a finished body-in-white, it looked like the legendary white whale due to its wide, low body shape

161 ■ 1

160 ■ 1

With Moby Dick, only the hard core of sheet steel remains from the Porsche 935 body. The racing department shaped the fenders, hoods, and aerodynamic components in plastic

161 ■ 1

From the side, Moby Dick reveals its second whale-like perspective; to achieve low drag, the body extends for a length of nearly 4.90 meters (16 ft)

162 ▪ 1

Dealing with a plentiful 900 bhp at speed called for massive tire dimensions, which caused Moby Dick's width to grow to 1.99 meters (6 ft 6 in)

163 ▪ 1

The flat six "boxer" engine with two turbochargers kept its air-cooled cylinders, but the four-valve cylinder heads were liquid cooled for the first time

163 ▪ 2

Besides the radiator for the new cylinder heads, Moby Dick also had an intercooler for the charge air from the two big turbochargers

163 ▪ 2

163 ▪ 1

on the race track, but from time to time at an earlier stage, by cunning interpretation of the rules. This is particularly true in Group 5, the class for the so-called "silhouette cars," which enjoy a great deal of technological freedom below the body, though this must at least have a certain similarity with the outline of the production cars.

At the time, Porsche had difficulty in getting approval for the low-slung nose on the 911's body. The company's rivals at BMW complained to the FIA about the rigid inviolability of the sills below the doors, since they wanted to put a tunnel through the one on the right side for an exhaust pipe.

As usual, this matter was submitted with the usual cry for justice. So BMW's advocates pleaded that BMW, with its front engine vehicles, had an unfair disadvantage against, and it would be very simple to move the exhaust pipe to the ideal spot.

A wise ruling by the commission in Paris accepted the tunnel and approved changes to the sills, whereupon BMW was finally able to lower the body of its CSL racing coupe way, way down.

At Porsche, racing engineer Norbert Singer was not at all horrified by the decision. He knew right away what was to be done: Porsche would also make use of the new freedom. He turned his racing department into a cutting department.

"We did not just cut away the sills," commented Singer on his team's daring moves in the Summer of 1977, "we simply took a whole slice out of the body at this level." The 911's body was lowered by 20 centimeters, but since the rules were changed in favor of BMW, the Commission was no longer able to do anything about the changes to the Porsche.

As long as the lowered 911 body was raised to working height on the assembly stand in the Racing Department, everyone thought it looked significantly lower and pretty wide, but not really unusual.

"Once the car was finished and we let it down, and it stood there on its tires all in white, unbelievably flat and quite wide, " remembers Norbert Singer with amusement, "we all thought it looked like the great white whale and somebody said in amazement: 'Hey, that's Moby Dick.' So our new car already had a name."

Just like a whale, the Porsche proved to be effectively streamlined over its entire body. Up front, it divides the air stream impressively with its wide front skirt. In the rear, like any good whale, it bears a wide tail fin, larger than any other racing Porsche with a 911 body had ever had. The purpose of this striking aerodynamic aid is by no means low drag, but rather the exertion of a powerful downforce, which provides a tremendous increase in ground contact as speed rises. It ensures that straight-line driving and cornering stability at speeds of up to 366 km/h (227 mph) are not left totally to chance. At that time, aerodynamic improvement of ground contact and roadholding was solely accomplished using wings attached to the body.

Norbert Singer comments on this: "It was not until later that we mastered the exploitation of the ground effect by designing the bottom of the car so that it creates an artificial vacuum at this point."

Beneath Moby Dick's flattened but heavily winged body burgeoned a whole crop of new technology. Amputation of the sills resulted in a loss of load-bearing elements, so the engineers were faced with the task of fitting the race car with a supportive corset. For this reason, they caused the roll cage (which was already present) to branch out towards the bottom to form a complete frame and used it to mount the suspension while they were at it. While its true that the seemingly strict sports regulations for these components calls for the same principle be used, the general freedom allowed in respect of springs and shock absorbers provided a good deal of flexibility – so the stabilizer bars used in the production cars vanished.

"There was nothing more we could do with them anyway,"

164 ▪ 1

164 ▪ 1/165 ▪ 1
At 366 kilometers per hour (227 mph), Moby Dick was the fastest whale on the Mulsanne straight in the 1978 Le Mans 24-hour race

explains Norbert Singer, "the thick stabilizer bars we needed for hard racing tuning no longer matched the other rear axle design elements." The heavy steel torsion bars were replaced with light coil springs made of titanium, threaded adjustably onto Bilstein gas-filled shock absorbers. This makes suspension tuning a quick routine job in the pit stop, with easy correction of the height and spring rate. Nevertheless, the basic design was not discarded. McPherson struts still guided the front wheels, and the path of the rear wheels was determined by heavily modified aluminum semi-trailing arms.

Still without any limits in the sports laws, Moby Dick wears the wheels and tires of 20 years ago in all their proud opulence. The 11 x 16 front rims are shod with size 275/600 - 16 racing tires. At the rear, where the turbocharged engine unloads its power, the rims are 15 inches wide and the diameter a forward-looking 19 inches. In keeping with these dimensions the tires were substantial too: 350/700-19. (To understand these racing dimensions: 275 or 350 indicate the width in millimeters; 600 or 700 the outside diameter in millimeters.)

The flatter body (which was by no means more aerodynamic) and the tauter suspension were not capable on their own of catapulting a Porsche 911 to a speed of 366 km/h (227 mph). Doing this required a revolution in the engine room which, as we now know, would take nearly 20 years to work its way from race car to series production.

Beginning with the conviction that four valves per cylinder are always better than two, the Porsche engineers concerned themselves with doubling the number of valves early in the 1970s. Nevertheless, the first air-cooled four-valve cylinder heads – even though similar ones were still being used successfully on racing motorcycles – proved unsuitable for the thermal loads in a racing car "which on top of everything else also had turbochargers." This is because when the number of ports is doubled the four-valve cylinder heads no longer have space for the required number of cooling ribs for heat removal.

Ad so the engine makers in Weissach risked the first step away from their traditional path of air cooling. They designed water-cooled cylinder heads with double overhead camshafts and four valves per combustion chamber. The first guinea pig for the new technology was a character already connected with the moist element: Moby Dick, the white whale.

For the water-cooled cylinder heads, the Racing Department designed a short block with every hint of concealed, violent power. A 95.7-millimeter bore and a stroke of 74.4 millimeters results in a displacement of 3,211 cubic centimeters. The six individual cylinders are still cooled by air from a horizontally rotating fan. Two turbochargers from the Kühnle, Kopp und Kausch company in Frankenthal, Germany deliver air to the cylinders via charge-air intercoolers at a pressure of two bars. At 6.5 : 1, the calculated compression ratio remains relatively low.

Nevertheless, since the turbochargers put a lot more air into the combustion chambers than a naturally aspirated engine can inhale, the effective compression ratio of 10 : 1 is considerably higher.

In the power output area, the technical documentation for this engine contains entries that are conspicuously crossed out. The last version of the corrections shows the value as 845 bhp at 8,200 rpm. Yet 20 years later, Norbert Singer says: "go ahead and write 900, the figure is by no means exaggerated."

In Moby Dick, this pure power melts together supremely with 1,025 kilograms (2,260 lb) of thoroughly stripped down 911 to provide tremendous performance. At high speed, the experience of driving the car is – as Schurti explained so clearly – more than a little awe-inspiring. This is due to the fundamental fact that all the changes to various parts of the chassis failed to disturb the original wheelbase of 2,279 milli-meters (89.7 inches). Moby Dick's power not only brings certain risks with it, but also some all too obvious side effects. A 120-liter tank (31 US gallons) gives a vague impression of the kind of thirst that the white whale was prone to have. These large reserves only lasted for a racing distance of 200 kilometers (124 miles), corresponding to just under or just over an hour of driving, depending on the circuit.

When describing the transmission, the specification sheet arouses the strong suspicion that a technical error has been made. Four-speed transmission is written there in a very matter-of-fact manner, which – for a car that reaches 366 km/h (227 mph) – seems pretty out of place.

Those who raced the car, however, had little reason to complain about the fact that the Super-Porsche had the same low number of gears as a Volkswagen Beetle. The reason for this is the remarkable flexibility of the racing engine with its unbelievable torque. The high mean effective pressure delivers a walloping 736 Newton-meters (543 lb.ft) to the crankshaft of the "boxer" engine at 5,600 revs. With this much propulsive force and a wide usable engine speed range, four gears are sufficient to tackle any race. In the light of such violent load reversals, however, it is astonishing that a single-disk clutch with sintered-metal facing is obviously so well able to withstand the onslaught of 736 Nm of torque.

Further down the driveline, examples can be found of simplicity, which sometimes borders on brutality. Moby Dick differs from the majority of cars, fast or otherwise, in everyday life by simply not having a differential. Instead, it has a rigid drive-through to the rear wheels. The engineers are more than happy to live with the unavoidable tension between the wheels when cornering in order to gain the positive effect of a one hundred percent differential lock. Traction is terrific, despite the powerful torque. Furthermore, the rigid driveline, with its built-in tendency to encourage understeer,

minimizes the potent rear-engined car's equally natural tendency to oversteer.

It is the mechanics who are more likely to have problems with Moby Dick's rigid driveline when they maneuver the car in the confined spaces of a pit lane or competitor's paddock. This is because when the full torque is not tearing at the rear wheels, the Porsche 935's turning circle is much bigger than that of the genuine white whale.

The Moby Dick from 1977/78 entered history as the fastest Porsche to wear the clothing of a 911. In the 20 years that ensued, there was never a more powerful car of this kind. This circumstance was not due merely to Porsche's own engineering decisions but to the strict restrictions imposed by motorsport regulations in the interests of safety.

Yet the success rate on the bottom line for possibly the most powerful (and as a result most famous) Porsche of all, the 935, does not match up to its reputation for being so full of sound and fury. Since Porsche left the fight for the 1978 World Manufacturers' Championship to the private entrants, Moby Dick remained a car for special races. Of these, however, it was only able to end one with success.

With it, Jacky Ickx and Jochen Mass won the six-hour event in Silverstone, England. Yet at the 24-hour race in Le Mans, Moby Dick was denied the heroic victory it sought. Plagued by persistent technical problems, Rolf Stommelen and Manfred Schurti were only able to take the low-slung coupe to eighth place. After that, the white whale was never quite itself again. Moby Dick is now locked up securely in the museum. From that time on, right up to 1981, races were won by simpler, air-cooled Porsche 935s.

With Moby Dick, the virus of water cooling began to creep up on the classic 911. Surprisingly, it took another 20 years for it to gain a place in series production.

TWO THIRDS OF THE LIMIT

by Rolf Kunkel

956/962

NEXT TO THE EMPTY STANDS of the "Circuit du Val de Vienne," in the middle of the undulating grasslands of Central France, stands a lonely emergency vehicle with a crew including a surgeon and two ambulance men. A half dozen race officials have taken up position along the circuit, and up in the tower, every meter of asphalt is being monitored by camera. You never know what might happen when one of the fastest racing cars ever built gets on the track.

For ten years, the blue-white-and-red racer with start number 17 stood motionless in the Porsche Museum in Zuffenhausen. "Now it's getting another chance to show what it can do," says museum director Klaus Bischof, who himself had been involved in the car's earlier competition activities, and does not let the car out of his sight now for a single moment. He refers to it as a legend, a racing car that set new standards in every way, and was the absolute embodiment of top speed in the 1980's. "It's worth the trip just to hear the sound of the engine."

This is not the tamed road version of the 962. This is the genuine article. The car that won Le Mans in 1987 . It has 680 horsepower on tap, and is so fast that it can travel 350 kilometers (217 miles) in an hour on the highway. The car was driven by Derek Bell, Hans-Joachim Stuck and Al Holbert, who crossed the finish line back then with an astounding twenty-lap lead over the team that finished second. It was probably Porsche's greatest Le Mans success, since it was the least expected too, after the race had begun with a catastrophic start.

The low-slung fixed-roof coupé, that cannot disguise the many hours it spent in the wind tunnel, with its 17-inch wide Dunlop tires and the long tail typical of Le Mans entries, still looks like a real race car today.

All told, 176 of these cars were built and sold to private customers. The final selling price was no less than 1.5 million German Marks.

Several mechanics from the old days have turned up at the circuit, and also some former drivers, such as Harald Grohs – "I have so many pleasant memories of the 962." Of course, gray-haired designer Norbert Singer, is present too. He takes a satisfied look at his masterpiece, the car he put on the Le Mans starting line in 1982 after a development period of just nine months. It took the first three places right away. Nothing like that had ever happened before. Remembering how his cars saw off the competitors one after the other, he grins. "Well, we seem to have had a slight edge in aerodynamics."

The circuit is 3.7 kilometers long, full of curves, and hard to follow. Bob Wollek, a driver from the Porsche works team, thinks it's great.

Bob, who was born 54 years ago in Strasbourg, and is one of motor racing's last dinosaurs, has the job of introducing me to extraterrestial driving. With his grey-streaked temples and wiry figure without a single ounce of excess fat, he looks like an aging jockey. He has stood on the victors' podium of a 24-hour race 47 times. By constantly experimenting around with a steady supply of new engines, new designs, and new tires, he has advanced into realms of expe-

170/171 ▪ 1

*On the road again – after a ten-year
sleep in the museum.
The car that won the 1987 Le Mans
24-hour race. Driven by Bell, Stuck
and Holbert, it crossed the finishing
line with a 20-lap lead over the
second-placed team*

173 ■ 1

rience that progress well beyond the imaginable. They are are so intensive that they cannot be compared with any other experience. "If you have never sat sat in a racing car before, you may be in for a surprise," he had said earlier during the briefing. One time a guy threw up all over his dashboard. That is why he did not propose to take the car all the way up to its limit. Even so, he promises, I will still get a chance to sample some of the sheer terror and the satisfaction that this sport brings with it.

Lost in thought, the quiet, taciturn man from Alsace takes a long look a the super-fast racer with which he celebrated the greatest successes of his carreer. He estimates that he has driven about 90,000 kilometers (approx. 55,000 miles) in the car, and every time he did something totally irrational. Wollek knows the 962 better than any other driver, including Jackie Ickx, Stuck, Mass and all the other big names from the Group-C era that made it the absolute victory car that ran for over a decade and wrote history year after year. In the fast life of racing, in which a new model arrives on the market practically every year, that is an unbelievably long time.

The driver's hands wrap around the rim of the small leather steering wheel. It has been ten years since he sat in this thing. A tremendous feeling. Mastering the 962 is like suddenly having a penis that's five centimeters longer. Just entering this car in a long-distance race, he says, was half way to winning. The rest was teamwork and luck. "In Le Mans, we didn't open the rear hood once in the whole 24 hours. We just filled up the tank and changed the tires, nothing else. You didn't have to worry about problems with the gear shift, or that the brakes would fail. You could simply concentrate on driving."

Bob is completely relaxed now, as he rests in the bucket seat and exudes a mildly casual aura that is presumably meant to encourage his passenger. Just one quick signature that frees the manufacturer of any liability in the event of an accident. The very fact that I agree to go along for the ride in this vehicle, which is on record as having a top speed of 395 km/h, shows how a missile like this can cause you to lose your senses.

Climbing in. You really ought to practice this a few times in seclusion before attempting it in public. That would spare you the mocking laughter of the mechanics as you attempt to fold your legs and body in such a way that everything fits into the tight carapace. Your legs are gripped like a vice, and your upper body is pressed close to the driver as if you were about to leave for your honeymoon.

Ready to go. The butterflies in your stomach flap their wings harder. The car lets out a few dry coughs as the rust is blown out of the pipes. In just a moment the two turbochargers start to supply full boost, which is then followed by a happening that cannot be described with the word "start". It's more like being shot onto the track, and it is accompanied by a noise like a tornado gathering momentum. Verbal communication is impossible. Tremendous power slams me backwards against the fuel tank firewall to which the water-cooled flat-six "boxer" engine is bolted.

Driving experience of the kind gained in my VW Golf is, in a word, worthless. Just a moment ago we were at a standstill, now we have reached one hundred kilometers per hour. In 2.6 seconds. No more than the blink of an eye. Five seconds later, we are already traveling twice as fast, and immediately we can see the first bend form on the cross-hairs between the two crouching front fenders. Close to the ground, your eyes at a truck's axle height, every change of direction is a strength test for the arm and shoulder muscles. The enormous centrifugal forces cause your head to swing back and forth helplessly, and the chassis presses up through the flesh and reaches the bones. Right after that, you get a real piece of Le Mans atmosphere: a long, almost perfectly straight road that reminds you of the famous Les Hunaudières, on which this car reached the 360 to 370 mark in the 1980's, lap after lap for 24 hours.

174 ■ 1

174 ■ 1

For Bob Wollek, the Porsche 962 is an old acquaintance. He estimates that he covered more than 90,000 kilometers (55,000 miles) in it

174 ■ 2

A workplace with a high-tech atmosphere – and yet the car with design number 962 was among the most reliable cars with a Porsche badge ever to be entered for a race. Bob Wollek: "In Le Mans, we didn't open the rear hood once in the whole 24-hours"

The car is now in its highest gear. It is impossible to say how fast we are going. It feels as if your unfortunate backside is being pulled out from under your body. As an organism, your body struggles to deal with the strange acceleration signals transmitted by pressure receptors on the skin and by the effects on the canals of the inner ear, which are thrown totally out of balance. Several things now happen at once. The spine sends out shock signals, the nerves of the muscle system react momentarily in the form of cramp. The central nervous system puts the entire body on alarm. You are not afraid, but inwardly, you are extremely tense.

For the person who normally drives a street-legal car, a totally new quality of perception now begins. At speeds of 260 to 270 km/h (160 to 165 mph), your brain, no longer able to process the rapid signals pouring in from the eyes, gives up trying and automatically switches to tunnel vision: the field of view reduces to what is absolutely necessary, directly in front of the eyes. Left and right are obliterated. Trees, straw bales and guard rails all veer away to one side or the other.

Speed itself is not the problem. The problem is controlling it. Destructive forces, technical defects, and driving errors that can deliver some nasty surprises, all develop in direct proportion to the acceleration. The stacks of tires at the end of the straits now whisk into view, and – almost miraculusly – stay where they are. The way that Bob Wollek goes into the bend proves that he must have grown up with the maxim: "He who brakes, loses." You expect some braking, a feeling of deceleration, but it never comes. There are hardly any intermediate stages. The 962 hurtles around the corners as though it were not a car on four wheels. It rides as though it were running on rails, and develops a phenomenal level of transverse acceleration.

Of course, as a passenger, you have no steering wheel in front of you. That makes the whole thing harder to deal with. You have no conception of how well the car handles. When you drive it, there must be a fantastic feeling when the car

begins to slide and you are just able to get it back under control. You know exactly when the four rubber surfaces that hold the car on the track are still in contact with the road, and when they are not. Around this corner at 185 km/h, around the other at 218.

The trick, if we may call it that, is to drive the car – which moves partially forwards and partially sideways – at an average of over 200 km/h (124 mph), lap for lap, close to its limits, with the greatest possible precision. This is a difficult skill to learn, because you cannot do it in a slower vehicle.

In order to get everything I could out of the experience, I had put a notebook in my pocket. I thought naively that I could jot down some thoughts underway, thoughts that might otherwise be lost forever. Instead, I end up grabbing hold of the cockpit with both hands and not letting go. What must this be like when there are another thirty such rockets on the circuit, all fighting for a square inch of ground?

On the third lap, something one might call the thrill of speed actually does arise. Suddenly all physical discomfort disappears. The trip starts to be fun. I'm overcome by a feeling of happiness. This is great, I can't believe I'm getting a chance to experience this! It is a strangely elevated, surreal and floating condition that I would be perfectly content to live in for the rest of my days. But all too soon, the long straight awakens me violently out of my dreams. Bob is even faster than he was on previous laps. This no longer has anything in common with driving a car on the highway, no matter how fast.

Enough is enough. Acceleration and braking in such rapid succession are beginning to have a numbing effect. Yet I am thankful to have had a chance to penetrate even slightly into a world in which the hardest decision to make is whether to put the car into second or third gear.

"Was that more or less racing speed?" is all I could stammer. "About two thirds," Bob replies in his quiet, never-waste-a-word manner, and looks over at me in amusement.

CHAPTER 7

Today

A new era began for Porsche in November 1992. The technical team at the Weissach Development Center submitted a revolutionary technical concept that drew a firm concluding line under many a hallowed tradition. It meant the end of the road for the no longer quite so young 968 and 928, and a total breakaway into the future with two new models, each a pure-bred Porsche. It meant rediscovering the trail that led from the historic Spyder to the new, youthful Boxster, and reincarnating the classic 911 in modern form.

With simultaneous engineering methods and a totally new production structure, Porsche has since 1993 been striding ahead along the successful road to the next millennium. Lift-off was instant when the Boxster was launched in 1996. A year later, the rocket's second stage was ignited in the form of the new 911, another sales success that has boosted car output to undreamed off-levels.

DR. WENDELIN WIEDEKING
With a keen eye for technical competence and economic efficiency, Wendelin Wiedeking has propelled Porsche back into the overtaking lane with immense vigor

911
The latest 911, in classic style but with leading-edge technical features

PRODUCTION
Porsche's production methods have grown younger with the times

WEISSACH
Horst Marchart runs the Development Center: he has been with the company since 1962. If the 911 were a man, this would be that man!

The Long Road from Craftsman to Robot

By Clauspeter Becker

Porsche in Zuffenhausen, yesterday and today

IN THE BEGINNING, THE WORLD WAS EMPTY. Fifty years ago, the young Porsche company was faced with the question of how to become a

178•1

world-famous car manufacturer without even having a factory. The cell from which the corporation developed in the town of Gmünd, Austria – where the Number 1 and a further 52 Type 356s were built in 1948, was no more than a small, shut-down saw mill. The Stuttgart property from the days of Volkswagen development work had been

seized by the American occupying forces, but in any case it was hardly suitable to become the company's Plant 1. What does an intelligent businessman do in a situation like this? He looks for a partner. And since Ferry Porsche knew that car making is predominately body making, he selected the long established Reutter coachbuilding plant in Stuttgart to be the workbench for his sports cars. This company had already been one of the Porsche design office's suppliers in the pre-war days.

In the summer of 1949, a rental agreement was signed with Reutter, for a 500 square meter (5,380 square feet) production workshop. The rent was 500 German Marks per month.

In November 1949, the first firm order was placed for 500 car bodies.

This car factory on Augustenstrasse,

surrounded by residential housing, was a long way from matching the size of other mid-20th century automobile manufacturing operations. And yet the little factory was capable of producing things of even much greater size. The Stuttgart streetcar authorities had Reutter produce and repair its vehicles. There was even a rail connection to make the deliveries.

As the Porsche marque became successful, the Reutter plant in the suburb of Zuffenhausen also joined the production scheme. Knowing that they shaped the rise of the Porsche marque out of sheet metal, working diligently with their own hands, gives the Reutter people a high degree of self-assurance. But after 40 years of Porsche sheet metal, each of them still says, "I'm a Reutter man."

By today's standards, it was still a craft trade that was performed in the dark halls of the 1950s. They did have mechanical presses, but what came out of them was not finished and ready to use. "The panels had to be smoothed out," says Roland Bemsel (59), who moved from production to the Racing

178•2

178•1

In the early years of Porsche, the hammer was used for more than just "ennobling" a car with a few taps on its badge

178•2

For many years now, every new Porsche has had to take a shower. The roof must be absolutely leak-proof

179•1

At the end of the final assembly line, every Porsche rolls through a solarium. In the light from these fluorescent lamps, the skilled craftsman can find every flaw

Department a long time ago, in an attempt to explain in modern terms. "You ought to know that it's called planishing," corrects his colleague Karl-Heinz Walter, who last year cele-

already an issue 45 years ago when I started my apprenticeship with Reutter. They were never right. We had to fill them afterwards with solder, Foreman Bemsel rembers, and Foreman Walter

nomic miracle", Porsches could only be made with a lot of manual effort. Reutter was unable to train as many body makers as it needed. "We had to teach people actually on the job," says Werner Gierl, a Reutter man since 1957, "but that was no problem even if they came from another trade, since they always had a sound attitude as far as good work and quality were concerned."

"But the people mocked us none the

180 ▪ 1

180 ▪ 2

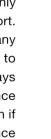

180 ▪ 1
The welds on a Porsche 356 were exceptionally long, and brazing work was also performed at difficult spots, all without any gloves, protective helmets, or goggles

brated his 40th anniversary in the workshop for the restoration of old-timers.

Forty years ago, the craftsmen's working hours (at 1.30 German Marks per hour) flowed into the production in altogether large numbers. "The rear sections of the car body were brought into shape by two workers. They were able to produce four in a nine-hour day," reports Gerhard Fellmeth, who joined the company in 1958. "The joint gaps were

recalls contentedly: "We could easily put 12 kilos (26.5 pounds) on the weight of a Cabrio."

It took hard work to smooth down the unevenness in the body (particularly around the many, long welds) using a sheet-metal plane. "Occasionally," reports Paul Fleischmann, who has been working in the production area since 1958, "the panels were planed almost all the way through."

In the early years of Germany's "eco-

less," remembers Werner Gierl with a smile. "They used to say: 'Reutter's inspectors are butchers, tailors, and barbers'."

Wolfgang Leimgruber (38), who has not been around long enough to be part of the Reutter tradition, is now Manager of the Cost Center for Bodies-in-White/Paint. He never saw the artisan phase of Porsche's production. And the days in which presses still rumbled away forming sheet metal in the old Reutter

180 ▪ 2
The atmosphere in the cafeteria has since become a bit brighter. The workers at Porsche are still permitted a beer at lunchtime

181 ▪ 1
Robots move the steadily growing sports car through the production buildings, where car bodies were once carried by hand

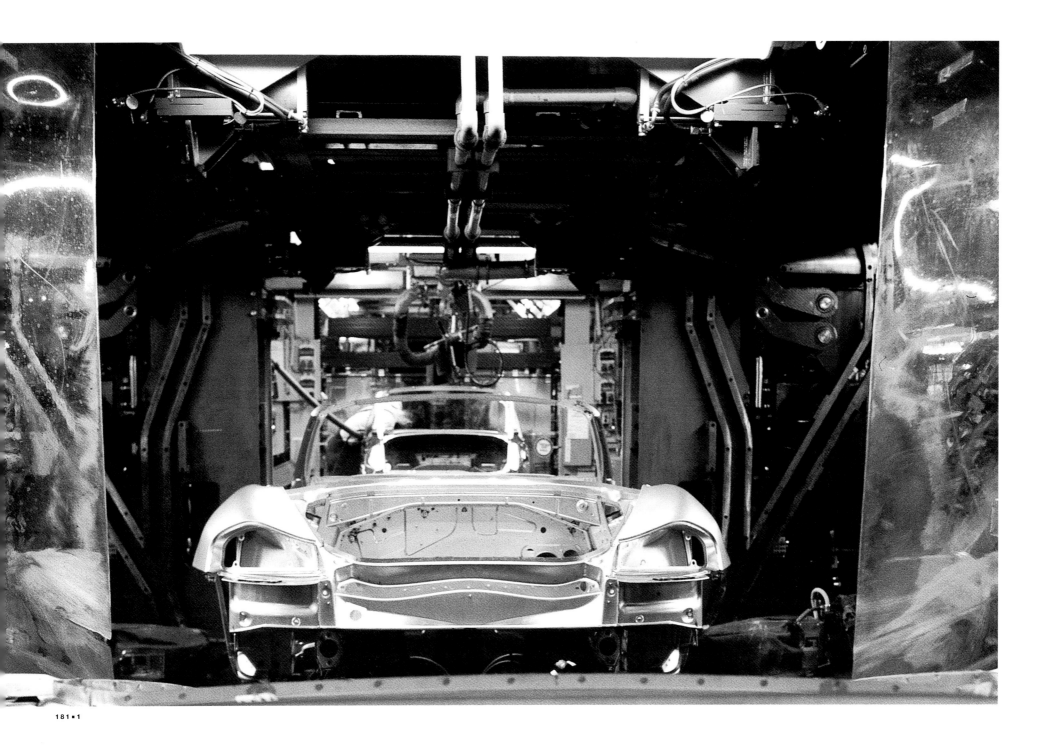

buildings are also long since gone. "Porsche has been buying in pressings from outside the company since 1973," Mr. Leimgruber explains. "Until the latest models they came from Allgayer, and now they come from BMW."

Body making has become more of an assembly operation, and has also been increasingly rationalized. As an example, Mr. Leimgruber points to door production: "One person operates a series of mostly automatic machines, and another is responsible for process control. On the last model, we still needed twenty workers for door production."

In 1988, it took 107 minutes to make a door, but by the time this door, which remain unchanged for nearly 35 years, finally went out of production the time had been cut to 70.85 minutes. Today, automatic machines fold and weld a door together every 13.96 minutes. The total body-in-white production time has been reduced from 28.9 hours (1986) to 15.35 hours (1998). The number of welds has gone down from 5,450 to 4,406, and the number of sheet metal pressings from 351 to 282.

Perfecting the production sequence was a tedious process, and a constant battle against the traditional urge to improvise. "When the Turbo was given flared fenders in 1974/75," recalls Karl-Heinz Walter, "at first, we simply added

182 ▪ 2

strips of sheet metal, and it was not until years later that we had wider fenders in a single piece."

"On all 911s until the 996, the front fenders were welded together from several parts, and then had to be smoothed – towards the end with electric tools, of course," says Wolfgang Leimgruber, recollecting the past.

"The work is easier now, and with the big presses gone, it is also a whole lot quieter," Horst Beutel comments, 42 years after he began his apprenticeship, "but we use to laugh more at work!"

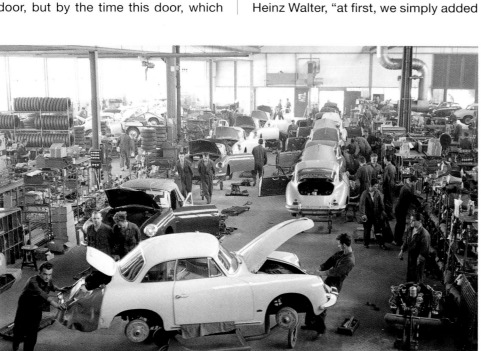

182 ▪ 1

182 ▪ 2 / 184 ▪ 1

In the early years of Porsche production, power train installation (known as the "wedding") was a primitive process, looking for all the world like traditional mechanical fitters in a small workshop

182 ▪ 1

There was no assembly line in the normal sense of the term in the first Porsche plant. During production, the cars were on "carts," which were pushed from one work point to the next. At 25 units per day, their rate of progress was still quite casual

183 ▪ 1-4

The majority of the welding work on a Porsche of the latest generation is performed with top perfection by an automated machine. This work used to be accomplished with spot welding tongs that weighed 40 kilograms (88 pounds)

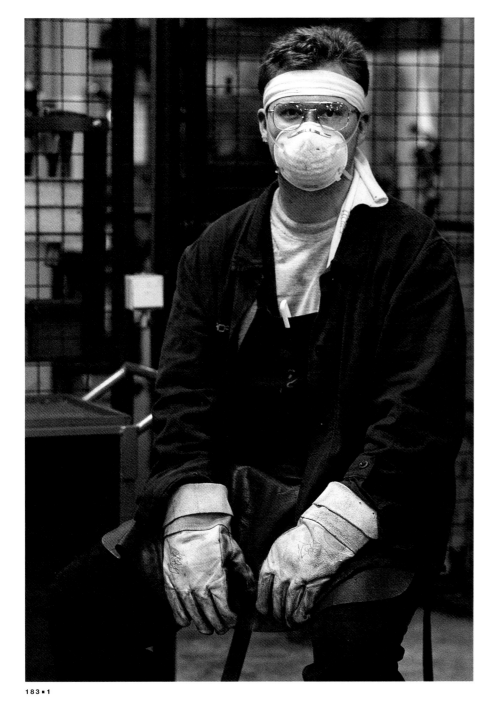

183 ■ 1

183 ■ 2

183 ■ 3

183 ■ 4

184▪1

185▪1

With new parts, the anatomy of the flat-six engine remains valid for the next generation of Porsches

185▪2

In modern modular production, the engine, transmission, and rear axle are put together on a side assembly line and later "wedded" to the body as a complete unit

185 ▪ 1

185 ▪ 2

185

By David Staretz
Photos by Aleksandra Pawloff

Where Porsche Lives

High-tech with a heart, or: holding the fort in Weissach

FRAU OPDERBECK knew what was going on right away before I even new what she was saying to our photographer: "A revolution! The collapse of the Cartesian view of the world. Your talented namesake was not right with his conditioned reflexes – animals think in a much more complex way than we believed until now. I haven't irritated you, have I Ms Pawloff?"

Hm. If this is the kind of eloquent greeting we can expect from the executive secretaries, what will it be like talking to the boss? Will he begin with the "World as Will and Idea"?

Horst Marchart
is Chief of Research and Development in Weissach, "a big shot," but a true top manager in the best sense of the term: relaxed, calm, candid, and as receptive as a sheet of paper.

*Do you remember your first day
at work?*
Yes, very well. The first of May, 1960. I arrived with my leg in plaster, following a skiing accident. I started in the Design Department, Engine Development section, then switched over to Contract Development, in other words automotive work for outside companies. But I was also in sales and a project manager for work we did with Airbus and with McLaren.
In 1971 I also became Technical Manager, in 1980 I went back to our Internal Development department and 1991 I became a member of the board.

*What kind of career training did
you receive?*
My technical training took place at the TGM, then I joined the Steyrwerke in Austria for two years, and from there I came directly to Porsche where I have been ever since.

*Was that your dream as a young
man?*
After two years at Steyr I wanted a change. I wanted to make engines: attractive, fast, powerful engines, and among the various companies in the German-speaking world, Porsche was naturally the best address.

*What opportunities does Weissach
have to offer?*
From the first sketch to the start-up of production we can do practically everything here that a development company has to do before series production starts.

We offer the same services to outside clients – with other automotive companies we do more than 140 million German Marks worth of business, and the tendency is still upward. I am also responsible for our racing activities. Everything that has to do with racing is under my authority here.

*Is there a special Weissach family
atmoshpere?*
I've been with the company for over thirty years. As far as the family atmosphere you mention is concerned, that's how it used to be. In the meantime things have become much harder and more profesional. The golden age of the chief engineers is over. Teamwork is now the order of the day, and this means that everything is handled with greater objectivity.

PEOPLE

187▪1
*Horst Marchart,
Director of Research and Development : "My father had a button-turning shop in Austria's Waldviertel area. It made mother-of-pearl buttons from fresh-water mussels"*

187▪2
*Günter Kern,
Manager of the Racing Workshop: "I was twelve years old when I first applied for a job at Porsche. The personnel manager nearly laughed himself silly"*

187■1

Does your position allow you to still have fun?

Sure, otherwise I wouldn't be here any more. It's not always fun – no more than 10 percent is creative, the rest is implementation at a high level.

Don't you get dizzy sometimes when you face decisions con cerning the far-distant future?

No, I have to say that I work very intuitively and use reasoning more as an aid – to see if it matches the intuition. And if it doesn't match, I think about it for a while longer. But I make decisions and take action relatively spontaneously.

Does that also mean that they are Porsche decisions?

I hope so, yes. My style has been shaped at Porsche, I can't deny that. Of course, I know what BMW or Mercedes would decide in my case, but to me, that is no more than collective criticism.

Do you come from a family of engineers?

Not at all. My father had a button-turning shop in the Waldviertel area of Austria.

187■2

What was your most memorable day at Porsche?

The day I was asked if I wanted to join the Board of Management. As an engineer, it was when we launched the 993. If it had not been built, I would probably not be here today.

Günter Kern

I've just returned from a test-drive session. It went well. Some of my colleagues were there for four days without a break. A 60, 70, or 80-hour week is quite normal.

At the moment the racing workshop is empty, and there are currently seven trucks on the road transporting racing cars to the Nürburgring, Paul Ricard and so on. Usually they all come back on Sunday evening, and you should see how hectic things are here on a Monday morning! In Le Mans, I'm responsible for logistics and for putting the vehicles together in the workshops, as well as for personnel planning on location.

How many people travel around?
There are 32 employees from the workshop alone. Nothing must go wrong, of course, because we have no replacements with us. The same number of engineers and racing technicians join us. Then we stage an unbelievable battle of resources. We arrive with five semi-trailers. One of the staff members just gave me the drawings for a new special truck. It's being built now, and has to be finished in three weeks. The trailer alone will cost 500,000 German Marks – without the content and the towing vehicle. Then we will have three-days at the most to set it up.
Those who work here in the Racing Department – Walter, come here for a minute! – know that it's a job like any other. Five semi-trailers, and everything has to be prepared.
I called Walter over because you asked who has golden hands here. Walter is one of our best, he is a Yugoslav, not that you'd notice. He designed this pit wagon here for instance, it's entirely his idea, and it is also used in the Super Cup Races at Formula 1 meetings. The tools inside it, four impact drivers, a fire extinguisher – everything you need – here is where the compressed air lines come out. As you know, electricity is not allowed in the pits because of the

danger of fire, and the whole wagon runs on cart tires. Walter is a typical Racing Department employee, someone who thinks for himself and comes up with ideas as good as this. People here don't keep looking at their watch, they see the job that needs doing, and that it has to be done, no matter how long it takes.

I take it there are not many family people working here?
Well there's me, for a start: I have my silver wedding anniversary next week.

Congratulations!
I'm 49 years old and have been with Porsche for the past 34 years. I have always been on the road. My wife has always backed me up, otherwise I would never have been able to do this job. Of course, we don't often get much time together …

How many racing weekends do you have each month?
In the peak seasons: four. Before Le Mans, for example, some of the team might not have a recovery phase for three months. They just have to do their best to lead a healthy lifestyle. We plan to give the assembly workers healthy food for the 24-hour Le Mans race. Professor Dungl, who is responsible for keeping the race drivers fit, is now compiling a meal-plan for the mech-

anics as well. We hope they will accept it. A lot of vegetables, a lot of herbs. Instead of Mars bars there will be fruit and grain balls.

How did you come to Porsche ?
I was twelve years old when I had my first interview at Porsche. My parents didn't know anything about it. The personnel manager nearly laughed himself sick when he heard that I wanted a job. A year later I came back; he recognized me right away and took down my personal particulars. in due course I was invited to take an aptitude test at the Stuttgart State Employment Office. There were a lot of people there who all wanted to take a test for Porsche. 'This is just great' I thought, they're only going to take twelve, and there are eighty people standing here!
After the test I went home sadly because I felt that I didn't have a chance. But – to my surprise – I got a letter saying that I was one of the twelve. I thought to myself: "This is the high point of your life, there's nothing more to achieve, you've reached the top." That's how happy I was!
First I did the apprenticeship and took the journeyman's test, then I wanted to go to the Repair Department, but they sent me to the Testing Department instead. That was 1965. I had long hair, but the people there were rather conservative; they wanted to cut my hair

189•1

Anthony R. Hatter, designer:
"Did you know that nearly everyone here – especially the designers – has a glass cabinet at home with Porsche scale models in it ? And a picture of them in their wallet!"

189▪1

right away with a pair of sheet metal shears. I was a wrestler at the time, Greco-Roman style, and things got physical real quick. After two weeks I was sick of the whole thing and went to the foreman to quit. But he just said: "Don't you have nothin' to do?" – "Sure I do," I said. "Then get about doin' it and shut your trap!" Which I did.

I became head assembler, group leader, master mechanic, chief master, and now workshop manager. I always made it to the next level, even though I never tried to get there.

I used to be in the Development Department, and when we drove the cars on endurance tests I used to think "Man, now you're a race car driver" – and everything worked out pretty well. I must admit I always thought "Now you've come as far as you can get", but strangely enough, there was always another step. But now I can't imagine a further step up. I want to be in charge here for a few years and turn the racing department into the model operation that it once was.

Then I'll be satisified.

Anthony R. Hatter

This Englishman has been at Porsche for ten years. In fact, it was the sight of a Porsche that first suggested to him that there must be something called car design.

After his technical training in Yorkshire, he went to a design school in Coventry and to the Royal College of Art in London. After a short spell at Opel (Porsche was already fully booked) he finally reached his true destination.

Back then, a lot of people came from Opel. The Weissach Design Studio is a smaller version of Ruesselsheim's Styling Center.

On my first day here, I was greeted by the secretary and by Mr. Lapine. Right away, I found myself at the dream spot for my dream job. I was also lucky enough to be able to work on dream projects.

My first job, however, was working on a sectional model of a 928 for the German Motor Show. But I was new back then: It was not until later that my talent came to the fore …

In 1989, Mr. Lagaay, our current boss, arrived and then we did the new 911. That was my first real project. It was very difficult. Grasping for the first time that one had to change the 911 … Crazy. Desecratation of the holy vessels ! We wanted to make a straightforward car without any unnecessary elements – a pure Porsche.

What does working here mean to you?

I can only try to describe it like this: I would find it very difficult to work anywhere else with the same motivation.

You're currently working on the GT1?
Yes, and the 911 Turbo.

What was your most memorable day at Porsche?
The greatest was the day that the GT1 went out for the first time. It was in the evening. Jürgen Barth was the test driver. The GT1 had been developed according to an extremely tight schedule. The first car was finished at 8:30 PM, and it was dark here in Weissach. The car had a dark carbon fiber color, very aggressive, and all together there were 50 people here. Everyone wanted to experience this roll-out. Then it came out onto the track. It was minus 5° Celsius (23° Fahrenheit) outside, the sky was crystal clear, and Barth drove it around the track. Then he came back into the slip road, the engine was switched off, and there was smoke and steam in the light from the big headlights – a close encounter of the third kind. Everyone walked up to the car slowly, and it was opened up in the front and back – everything was OK, so they screwed it back together and sent it back out onto the track. I still can't believe that somebody would roar around the track like that in a brand new car. For which I was partially responsible! Porsche! *(He shows us pictures of the complex design work done on the GT1).* It was the most in-tensive period of work in my life. Day and night, and at the weekends too.

This scratching away of the clay body – there's something about the process that's like archaeology.
If we say that, then we could dig way down, and then the Porsche 964 would come to light, the 911 that was built in the 1980s and shares the same under-pinning. The headlights were also borrowed from the previous car, so that we had something to start from.
(We look at a few Porsche models made out of metal, plastic, or chocolate).
Did you now that nearly everyone here in Weissach – especially the designers – has a glass cabinet at home full of Porsche models? And besides the pictures of their family, everyone carries a picture of their cabinet in their wallet: "Have you seen my cabinet?" Every corner of Weissach is filled with this kind of passion.

Wolfhelm Gorissen
I'm in charge of the Central Project Management Department. That's a very abstract term. We are a contract development department – we work for other companies – and also develop our own projects. These are always coordinated in the Central Project Management Department. We also provide managers for development projects, we look at the entire vehicle, perform overall testing, and draw up the concepts for new vehicles.
Although we take care of the project side of things, we pass on the actual work to what we call the line departments: Engine Design, Body Design … this is where it all comes together.

190 ▪ 1

190 ▪ 1
Wolfhelm Gorissen,
Project Management:
"By chance my daughter met an
American Porsche driver.
His parents were so excited:
A Porsche kid!"

We thought we would find a giant computer screen here.

I don't need that. We don't need a big central brain. We have a large Planning Department, which we can consider as a kind of central nervous system. Forty-five people work there on co-ordinating these projects. But there is no call for a giant computer.

Are there projects from other companies that you consider too small, or where would you draw the line and say that is not a job for Porsche?

It's not a matter of size, it's a question of subject matter. We don't tackle everything. For example, years ago there was a heart specialist – a famous man – who has since died. He said: "You guys make fantastic Formula 1 engines. You are the right people to design an artificial heart for me."
At first we said: "What a great job, here we have a chance to gain a few honors. That would be great."

Then we started to think about it and wrote the man a letter. We said we couldn't do it, since these biomedical factors, the related chemical factors, and the reaction of specific materials with the blood plasma, deposits, etc. – that is not our area of expertise, it would have taken us a long time to work our way into the subject.

A heart from Porsche – there must be people who couldn't imagine anything better.

We said the same thing, but when we took a closer look, it just wasn't a serious undertaking for us. So we turned it down.
Back then, when we were approached with the idea, I was still manager of the Contract Development Department. Of the entire capacity here at Weissach, about a third or a quarter is for Contract Development, in other words we make about a third of our capacity available to industrial customers.
There we make the most remarkable things: construction machinery, air-plane cockpits, totally new elevator systems … and cars as well. We prefer to do cars – for the international auto-motive industry. Or engine develop-ment for Harley-Davidson for example – it is all possible! Everything that mo-ves.
Two thirds of our capacity is devoted to the development of our own products. This percentage changes of course. Currently we have a lot of work of our own to do, so the amount we do for other companies goes down. Here in our own Development Department, we perform only car projects. And if we have the choice, we prefer to make only cars in our Contract Development Department as well.

What brought you here?

Me? I was a total car freak. I saw my first Porsche when I was 14 years old. It was a test car for Continental tires.
It parked in our village. I stood next to it with my bicycle and started up a con-versation with the driver. He told me he came by about every two weeks, but he normally took the by-pass. So for three whole weeks long I skipped school and lay in the grass waiting for this man to come back. That is how much the Porsche 356 had fascinated me. The man never came.
So I went back to school. But the idea had taken root. After my studies – auto-motive engineering, of course – I defini-tely wanted to go to Porsche. An Aus-trian hired me, Spieß, the VW engine designer. Back then we were all to-gether in Zuffenhausen. We moved out here in '74.

Is your job too much of a desk job for you, or do you still get a chance to roll up your sleeves?

I just came from a technical meeting. We were discussing the soft top de-sign. Our company still has a few such treats in store for its executives.
We've stayed a bit more firmly on the ground than a lot of other companies.

To what extent is Porsche inter-woven with your private life?

I met my wife through Porsche. I was at

191

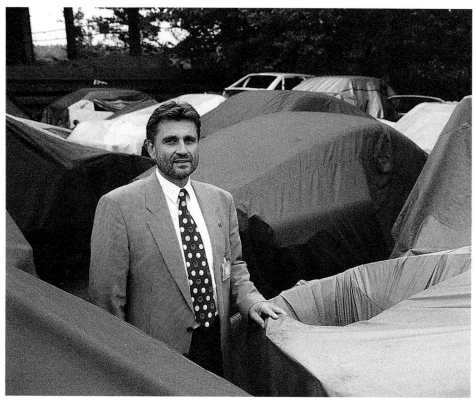

the Geneva Motor Show, and since the railroad system is so good in Switzerland, I didn't take the car. That's how I met my wife on the train. "People with brain travel by train," the Swiss say. As an automotive engineer I can't endorse that statement 100 percent, but in this case ...

My daughter met an American Porsche driver by coincidence. His parents got real excited when they realized: Wow, this is a Porsche kid!

It is difficult for a German to imagine how deep the Porsche loyalty is in America – it's unbelievable. My daughter was passed on from one Porsche family to another through the entire USA, from the St. Lawrence River via Chicago to California, and to Florida. With free flights – four months long. Something like that can only happen with Porsche. Since then, they have invited me as well.

Waldemar Wysocki

I'm Environmental Coordinator and Group manager for works security.

Altogether I have a staff of 20, including two ladies who receive guests.

I coordinate most of the work of the Environmental Protection Department in Zuffenhausen. We discuss every meas-

192■1

*Waldemar Wysocki,
in charge of plant security and
environmental protection:
"We sawed off Lehmann's
favorite branch of a tree on the
road that leads up to the factory"*

ure we implement: it goes through the Department, is discussed with the person responsible for Environmental Protection (who sometimes also presents it to the Board of Management), and then we try to put the whole thing into practice.

Does that mean that you don't need any ideas of your own?
We do have some ideas of our own! But we also have statutory regulations that we try to implement as best we can.

How does that look in practice?
I'm responsible for hazardous goods handling, prevention of water pollution, laser protection in Weissach, and also waste material handling. To do this, I attended various advanced training seminars ...

And then plant security to top things off – isn't that a bit too much?
Basically, it all happens at the same time. My job here is to ensure that no damage arises – whether through theft, outside influences, or negligence. When we make our rounds, we don't just check security-relevant matters, we check all the various plant facilities too. We check different areas to see if there are leaks or if anything else like that is going wrong.
Security requires more work on my part – as far as environmental protection is concerned, things run pretty much on their own, at least until new regulations come into effect.
Besides, I don't know anyone here in the company who only does just one job.
We have not had any cases of works

espionage, but when curious people "wander around," it's our job to escort them out politely.

And Lehmann (a well-known photographer and prototype hunter) *in the trees? What do you do about him?*
We are not really responsible for that, since it takes place outside the factory gates. But since you mention it – we sawed off one of his favorite branches on a tree where the road leads up to the factory!

By Emanuel Eckardt

Elan and Experience

A conversation with Porsche AG's Chief Executive Officer

HOW DO YOU GUIDE A GROUP OF COMPANIES? How do you traverse the dirt roads of a recession, accelerate production, pass the competitors, pull a corporation around the corners, and avoid the treacherous ditches of the economy? Accelerating, shifting gears, steering, braking, and finding an open space to park a few millions just at the right time? If only it were that simple!

Dr. Wendelin Wiedeking, 44, Chief Executive Officer of Porsche AG since 1992, is one of Germany's most successful businessmen. His success might not have been so spectacular had his company made diapers or for cat food, but the chief executive of Porsche AG is clearly obliged to stand in the public eye. He represents a top product that triggers emotions, creates excitement and provokes rejection. In this position, you can fall a long way. Wiedeking, who comes from the Westphalia region of Germany, is a fighter by nature. He took charge in difficult times, and forced through some painful cuts in order to achieve a success that is probably unique in Germany.

If we are to accept his view, there is no special secret to this success, apart from a lot of hard work. Yet it all would have been inconceivable without strategic thinking, without relishing the task, and without a degree of luck. What makes the man tick who will lead Germany's high-class sports car maker into the next millennium? This water-cooled meeting in the Board's offices in Zuffenhausen was not the first time we had met. The fact that I was given a "Group" answer to a personal question, came as no surprise.

How are you doing?
Well. Somewhere between well and very well. We are happy about the development of the dollar, yen, and pound. The number of orders placed for the Boxster and 911 has exceeded our wildest dreams. At the moment, we can't produce as fast as we can sell. That makes us content, of course, but it also has a negative side: our customers have to wait too long to get their cars. We have to solve this problem quickly.

How many cars do you produce?
We've set our sights on at least 38,000 for the 1997/98 fiscal year.

At least?
Let's just wait and see.

Then I'll ask you about some safer figures. When were you born?
On August 28, 1953, on the same day as Goethe, but a few years later.

Do you have any brothers and sisters?
I grew up with three siblings: one older sister, and two younger brothers.

Were you interested in cars as a kid?
Cars were always my hobby. As a child, I collected "Wiking" model cars. I still have them today, all kinds of them, at least 1,500. My grandmother in particular was always very generous to me.

What was your first car?
A pedal car that I received as a gift when I was a small boy. Then came a

"The attraction of the Porsche marque is immense. For most people, working for Porsche is a dream. I consider this emotional connection to be important. Our work, our preferences, and our hobby must blend together"

scooter, then a bicycle, and when I was 19, the first real car – a VW Beetle 1300. But I was already driving as a 14-year-old. I wore a large hat so that I would look bigger behind the wheel, since I could hardly see over the dashboard. Then I cruised around in my father's Opel Rekord. He didn't like that at all, by the way.

How did you get into the car making business?

When I was still just a boy, I built my own soap-box car. We ran them down the Beckum Hills. For a kid from the flat countryside, they seemed mighty high at the time. I'm still proud of that soap box today. I designed it with really complex steering and had the parts welded together by the local smith. For me, riding down the hill in my own car was a great feeling.

Did you experience a "speed high" in the soap box?

No. More on my bicycle. I always rode too fast, and frequently fell off. My knees had to be stitched up a few times.

Did you go in for sports?

The usual ones. Swimming and soccer, for example.

I assume you played in the attack?

I was a center forward.

196▪1

Were you a prize pupil?
No, I never wanted to be best in the class. At school, I was always one of the bad kids who sawed through the legs on the teacher's chair. My grades tended to be average. But when the time came to take the college entrance exams, I hit the spot. My scores in the critical subjects were just good enough for me not to have to take any oral exams. I think that annoyed some of the teachers.

Do you still remember what your average was?
Higher than a "B."

Were you ambitious?
I majored in mechanical engineering in Aachen. They expect a lot of you there. Their requirements were high in the basic subjects. After ten semesters, I had my diploma.

What was the subject of your dissertation?
Production engineering. It was about machine dynamics. But when I read it now, I can't imagine that I ever wrote it.

Did you work in your spare time while you were studying?
Yes, the whole time. I worked for a computer company. Then I tackled a few projects of my own. Since I wanted to be a mover and a shaker, entrepreneurial vision was always important to me. I started up four companies during that period. They're all still running today, incidentally. I was into real-estate for a while as well.

A wrong turn?
When I was a student, I had to pay a real-estate agent a 600-Mark fee. Then I saw her driving around in a six-cylinder BMW. I said to myself: "You can do that too."

Was money important to you?
It gave me the freedom to live differently from how I would have otherwise.

196

196•1

I never wanted to be best in the class. At school, I was one of the bad kids who sawed through the legs on the teacher's chair. My grades tended to be average. But when it came to taking the college entrance exams, I hit the spot. My grades in the critical subjects were just good enough for me not to have to take any oral exams. I think that annoyed some of the teachers!

I had to earn everything myself. My first piece of furniture was an inflatable mattress. It only had one problem: the air leaked out of it every night!

When did you sign up with Porsche for the first time?
I was 29 years old when I arrived in Zuffenhausen. I became a production management assistant. I was fortunate to be entrusted with a lot of responsibility while I was still young.

The headhunters in the branch had their eyes on you very quickly.
To what do you credit your success?
Primarily to hard work and commitment. I always tried to give my best.

Then you switched to the supplier industry …
Yes, there was an interesting job for me there, with a chance to take on responsibility in a leadership position. That appealed strongly to me then.

Was it easy? After all, you were still relatively young…
I was lucky. There was an older man on the staff there who taught me a lot. With his experience and my enthusiasm, we were able to crack open some of the stagnating structures.

What was your most important experience during this period?
I learned that you have to work hard on yourself. I also learned that you can't have it all at once as a young person. Today I know that success is a mixture of experience and enthusiasm.

Are you impatient?
Yes. But I've also learned that it's useless to take action so fast that the others can't keep up with you.

They say you're hard as a rock …
Not as much as I used to be …

Do you have a magic formula for leading people?
Not a magic formula. But I have learned from experience over the years. I now know when I can give my staff freedom. You always have to challenge your team, but you also have to give people freedom to develop their own abilities.

Are you distrustful of others?
To start off, I assume that everyone has good intentions. But I've learned to be more careful, I try to question more. Without a certain ability to judge character, it wouldn't be possible to do this job. You need psychological training in order to recognize patterns and structures, and to receive the signals people send with their body language. But in the end, I tend to trust my feelings.

Isn't there anyone you trust blindly?
Certainly there is; but only a very small number of people.

A handful?
Maybe ten. But this trust is one that has grown over years.

What does speed mean to you?
Speed means that you have to concentrate and anticipate. Your senses are sharpened, and you develop a totally different instinct for potential dangers that lie far ahead. You feel them without seeing them.

You identify yourself with your job.
With the Porsche marque as well?
The attraction of the Porsche marque is immense. For most people, working for Porsche is a dream. I consider this emotional connection to be important. Our work, our preferences, and our hobby must blend together.

THE GRACE OF PROGRESS MAKES
TRULY FINE CARS IMMORTAL

by Clauspeter Becker

996

THE 911 LIVED LONGER than all those meant to replace it, because it is the most unmistakable of all Porsches.

The 911 watched as its small four-cylinder colleague entered the world as the 924 and left it as the 968. It was too expensive to be a "sensible" car and too sensible to be an expensive one.

The big colleague with eight cylinders, known for fifteen years by the number 928, missed every chance to inherit the throne, because the true friend of the wealthy customer, the 911 Turbo, always resided permanently at the summit of the Porsche model line.

As a fair sportsman, the 911 waited until its other colleagues were ready to retire before beginning its second life.

On November 21, 1992, Hans Marchart, the member of the Porsche executive board responsible for engineering, defined the steep flight path for the launch of a new 911 generation with a long-term future. This engineer's concept included everything Porsche needed to succeed in the cost-oriented automotive industry. During his time, the engineers made the double decision: the smaller Boxster and the up-market 911 were to be based on the same technology. In February, this recipe for success – which has long since been realized – convinced the board of management. The 911's future and second career had begun.

And so a revolution begins to take shape. Nevertheless, certain appealing traditions, it was felt, should not be stamped out. In the design studio where Harm Lagaay and his team gladly tackled "the biggest job in the company's history," the 911's classic design was translated very carefully into the formal language of the late 20th century.

Harm Lagaay vividly illustrates what they were able to do: "We interpreted the sporting character that the 911 radiates in a new and elegant way. The last old-style model, with its flared fenders, had a muscle-bound, aggressive appearance like Olympic athlete Ben Johnson; the new 911 is like the younger Carl Lewis – equally fit for high performance, but with a slimmer and much more evenly proportioned figure."

Behind the car's self-assured appearance, there has been real visual and technical progress: the stiff profile from the 1960's that dictated a rather steep windshield has made way for a flowing line. The flush-mounted side windows underline the smooth form instead of interrupting it. Aerodynamic drag is lower, and the lifting forces – which tend to raise a car on its springs at high speed – remain minimal.

Inside the new 911, the occupants have never had it better, no matter what hard-core critics choose to believe: there is a pleasing space bonus everywhere you look, and even the luggage does not have to be squeezed in quite as tightly as it once had to.

The long line of air-cooled forefathers – which got off to a historic start with the Volkswagen engine and ended with turbocharged 12-cylinder versions developing over a thousand brake horsepower – is now retiring after 60 years of devotion to the Porsche task. The two new Porsches again have horizontally opposed, flat-six "boxer" engines, but from now on, they will be water-cooled.

This principle, too, has a respectable heritage at Porsche

201 ▪ 1

TODAY
The new 911

200 ▪ 1

The roof follows a curve of perfect harmony between the windshield and the engine hood. Heat from the vigorous "boxer" engine flows out of the grill on the hood after each drive

201 ▪ 1

After the 80 kilometer per hour (50 mph) mark is passed, the rear spoiler comes out of its hiding place and grabs the air to provide the safety of firm ground pressure and tire grip

202 ▪ 1

The new Porsche – perfect in profile and proportions. The fact that it has grown (to provide space for the radiators and trunk, and for added passive safety) is hardly noticeable

203 ▪ 1

The wheels are now even bigger. The standard alloy rims have a diameter of 17 inches, and for a real touch of style the new 911 can be had with optional 18-inch wheels

203 ▪ 1

– a heritage that includes more than just the discontinued four- and eight-cylinder engines. The TAG engine, which was decorated with the world championship title, cooled its cylinders with liquid – as did the six-cylinder "boxer" engines that took off year after year to win the 24-hour race in Le Mans and other long-distance events.

Thus it was with the highest of qualifications that the engineers at the Weissach Development Center set about replacing the best "boxer" of all times with a worthy successor. It was to be slimmer – in format, weight, and costs.

Within this framework, the engine-makers put together a compact and progressive package: two camshafts on each side, variable opening times for the inlet valves, four valves per cylinder and spark plugs located efficiently in the middle of the combustion chambers. The two-part engine housing is made from the ideal material of our day, pressure cast light-alloy, with the oil in an integrated dry sump formed as a separate chamber in the engine block.

In this way, a "boxer" engine with brand-new punch was created, an engine that knows how to combine responsiveness with a walloping blow, like Cassius Clay in his younger years. With this new 3.4-liter design, Weissach succeeded in re-inventing the free-revving engine. The new limit is at a bold 7,300 revolutions per minute, and in order to generate its rated 300 bhp (221 kW) output, which is usually more than sufficient in practice, the crankshaft whirls diligently at 6,800 rotations per minute.

The young "boxer" has retained the old free-revving spirit. But below these exalted engine speeds, it also knows how to slam the power onto the road: with a maximum of 350 Newton-meters (258 lb.ft.) of torque available as low down the scale as 3,600 rpm, the 911 simply surges forwards.

Even below this, however, flexibility at the low end of the scale gives the new 911 the kind of relaxed, gliding elegance that was once the domain of opulent sedans.

All these qualities add up to a timeless machine. It combines the craving for high engine speeds that the wild old models had with the smoothness of a new, environmentally oriented generation.

The engine is an unsurpassed example of intelligent engineering with broad vision that is never fixated on just a single goal. On one hand, there is the new maximum power and torque, putting the 911's temperament pretty close to the raw power of the turbo. It now sprints from zero to 100 km/h (62 mph) in just five seconds. Yet despite the additional power, the "boxer" is not as uptight as it used to be. If you wish, you can make use of the six gears and the engine speed limit, but it is not a must. The six-cylinder engine is every bit as forceful at 1,200 revs per minute.

When it came to the suspension, the engineers again went for the doubly ambitious goal of being both universal and clearly better. They first confronted the 911 with the task of establishing a clear lead over its toughest competitor – the previous 911 – on the North Loop of the Nürburg Ring.

After two sets of tires had been worn down, the verdict was clear: the new model is eight seconds faster and can be driven with significantly less effort. The steering is more agile and acts with greater precision, the longer wheelbase calms things down on the straight and when drifting hard through fast curves close to the handling limit.

Nevertheless, since other highspots in the life of a Porsche do not take place on smooth asphalt, but on the more undualting pavé of side streets in French country villages, the Porsche engineers needed to show off all their skills in translating suspension travel into ride comfort. They selected some very sophisticated makes of car to serve as a standard. And having searched for and found this high level of comfort, it does not bother them at all when someone comments in amazement: "The ride is outstanding, just like a …!"

The new 911

*In the perfection of the pure
Porsche form, the new Cabriolet
surpasses all its predecessors.
As with the Coupé, the line of the
soft top flows in a harmonious arc
to the now more tautly rounded
form in which the tail conceals the
flat-six engine*

208▪1

*A hardtop for the perfect metamor-
phisis into a Coupé was part of the
design specification from the first
day of development on.
And Cabriolet customers do not
have to pay a single German Mark,
US dollar or whatever in addition to
get a solid roof over their heads*

209▪1

*The new soft top, which opens at
the touch of a button and promptly
disappears, leaving us surrounded
by the perfumes of nature; one of
the most expensive options for a
911, but also one of the best*

209▪1

With this ambitious goal of not just going faster, but also doing everything else better than any 911 before it, the latest 911 is its own best ambassador for establishing diplomatic relations with new groups of buyers. A sport package rewards the iron men of yesterday with even better times on the Nürburg Ring. The new 911, with internal development number 996, was better prepared for all its future roles than any previous Porsche. The open-top version was not developed after the fact, as is usually the case; this time, it grew up along with the fixed-roof version right from the start.

The result is an open sports car with no hint of compromise. When folded, the soft top disappears entirely from the scene, and no longer remains perched on the tail like a forgotten piece of luggage.

The roof dips ingeniously under a flap in such a way that the firm, outside surface of the fabric remains exposed. The folding procedure is the same as has proved so successful on the Boxster, the only difference being that the 911's larger roof needs an additional fold. Nevertheless, lowering the soft top is not in the least complicated for the driver: a microprocessor issues commands to the electric motor and ensures that they are carried out correctly.

Beneath the large canvas roof and behind the four side windows of the new 911 Cabrio, there is an agreeably generous helping of tradition. Like the majority of all Porsche Cabrios in the past 50 years, the latest open 911 has two seats in the back to create an appropriate natural habitat for acclimatization of the next generation of Porsche drivers.

Personal thanks from the photographer and authors to the people, companies and other organizations who helped with their very special kindness and skill:

Special thanks to Dr. Ing. h.c. F. Porsche AG and
Studio Bastille • Klaus Bischof • Pascal LeCossec • Hervé Fontaine • Wolfhelm Gorrissen • Anthony Hatter • Hans Herrmann • Anton Hunger • Kunstmuseum Bonn • Herbert Linge • Horst Marchart
Hans Mezger • Klaus Parr • Mansour Ojjeh • Spedition Küke Motorsport GmbH • Karl-Friedrich Scheufele • Norbert Singer • Klaus Steckkönig • Vitra Museum/Weil am Rhein
Dr. Wendelin Wiedeking • Bob Wollek • Waldemar Wysocki

Photo Credits

All color photos: Peter Vann, except pages 128-131 (Porsche Archives)
Black & white photos: Porsche Archive and Aleksandra Pawloff for the "People in Weissach" contribution (pages 186-193)
Illustrations on pages 76-83 by Serge Bellu, illustration on page 86 by Studio Farr